THE WALL STREET JOURNAL.

NATIONAL BUSINESS EMPLOYMENT WEEKLY

Premier Guides

RESUMES

THE NATIONAL BUSINESS EMPLOYMENT WEEKLY
PREMIER GUIDES SERIES

Published:

Resumes,   ISBN# 0-471-31029-8 cloth;
                      ISBN# 0-471-31028-X paper

Interviewing,   ISBN# 0-471-31024-7 cloth;
                      ISBN# 0-471-31025-5 paper

Networking,   ISBN# 0-471-31026-3 cloth;
                      ISBN# 0-471-31027-1 paper

Forthcoming:

Cover Letters,   ISBN# 0-471-10671-2 cloth;
                      ISBN# 0-471-10672-0 paper

Alternative Careers, ISBN# 0-471-10919-3 cloth;
                      ISBN# 0-471-10918-5 paper

THE WALL STREET JOURNAL.

NATIONAL BUSINESS EMPLOYMENT WEEKLY

Premier Guides

RESUMES

Taunee Besson

John Wiley & Sons, Inc.
New York • Chichester • Brisbane • Toronto • Singapore

Library of Congress Cataloging in Publication Data:

National Business Employment Weekly.
   Resumes / by National Business Employment Weekly.
     p. cm.
   ISBN 0-471-31029-8 (alk. paper).—ISBN 0-471-31028-X (pbk. :
alk. paper)
    1. Résumés (Employment) I. Title.
HF5383.B44 1944
808'.06665—dc20   93-49882

Printed in the United States of America

10 9 8 7 6 5 4 3 2 1

Foreword

Job hunters often believe they have little control over how hiring managers perceive their resumes. Fortunately, that premise isn't true. Although your resume will likely receive no more than a 30-second review, in that brief time it can effectively sell your credentials and experience to cautious company recruiters.

To be sure, writing a great resume is hard work. The competition is fierce since most of the job hunters you're competing against have access to computers and can experiment with styles and typefaces. While your options may seem overwhelming, the alternative—following old rules or simply adding your latest job to an outdated resume—isn't adequate. It's critically important for you to spend time building a resume that reflects both your unique experiences and your potential contributions if hired. That's where this book comes in handy.

Career counselor Taunee Besson has helped thousands of job hunters write winning resumes. The key, she says, is to determine what you want to achieve, then construct a resume that addresses a recruiter's primary concerns while also meeting your career objectives. She describes this approach in the pages that follow, and does so very effectively.

Taunee starts by explaining the role of resumes in the search process and helps you organize the data you'll need to include. She reviews the basic ingredients that hiring authorities hope to see and shows how you can grab their attention without coming on too strong. Taunee then examines the different types of formats, offering pros and cons for each style, and analyzes specific resume approaches recommended for a variety of candidates ranging from first-time job seekers, women returning to the job market, career changers and older applicants.

Taunee's book is crammed full of actual resumes from successful candidates nationwide. By using this book in your campaign, perhaps you'll have a new resume worthy of inclusion in a future edition.

TONY LEE
Editor
National Business Employment Weekly

Acknowledgments

Many people have been very helpful as I put this book together. While I cannot name them all, I'd like to thank Tony Lee and Perri Capell for choosing me to write this book, and for their help editing it and soliciting sample resumes from readers. Many newspapers nationwide also published our request for great resumes, and these fellow journalists have my gratitude and a promise to return the favor should they ever need a little help from a friend.

I also want to recognize Jim Henry, Tom Arterburn, the staffs of Options Resource and Career Center in Houston and the Career Action Center in Palo Alto, California, as well as their clients, for contributing an excellent selection of sample resumes. They are responsible for many of the specialized examples in this book. Special thanks also to cartoonist Tom Cheney and Robert Half, the creator of Resumania, for their wonderful, humorous contributions to this book.

My own clients and newsletter readers deserve a tremendous thank you for allowing me to use their resumes, and for showing uncommon understanding when I needed to concentrate on the book instead of them. Richard Bolles has my gratitude for cultivating my healthy disrespect for run-of-the-mill resumes, and for inspiring my adaptation of his transferable skills exercise.

I also want to acknowledge the support of my family and friends who saw a lot less of me as this book came together. While they've always been sympathetic to my need to spend lots of time with clients and the community, this past year has demanded a level of forbearance verging on saintliness.

I dedicate this book to Larry, Amber and Teal Besson.

About the Author

Taunee Besson is president of Career Dimensions, a Dallas consulting firm that helps individuals and companies with issues such as career change, career pathing, small-business strategies, spouse relocation/employment and outplacement. She is a bimonthly columnist for the *National Business Employment Weekly,* and is a frequent speaker and guest author. Ms. Besson has taught courses at numerous Dallas-area colleges, and is an active community volunteer.

Contents

3 Resume Guidelines   45

4 The Parts of Your Resume   59

5 The Chronological Format   81

6 Functional Resumes   107

7 Hybrid Resumes   129

8 Resumes for Consulting, Freelancing, Volunteer and Internal Company Use   153

13 Electronic Resumes 241

14 Resume Follow-Up 251

Index 261

Introduction

Resume Angst . . .

"I would rather have a root canal than write another resume."

"I've been working on this resume day and night for the last two weeks and I'm not going to stop until I get it perfect."

"Frankly, I think that resumes are totally pointless. Why people bother to write them is completely beyond me."

"You and I both know a job search is strictly a numbers game. To get 5 interviews, I'll have to send out 500 resumes. To get 10 interviews, I'll have to mail 1,000."

"A resume should always have an objective . . . a resume should never have an objective. I read two different books and they give diametrically opposing advice. If the experts can't agree on something as simple as this, how am I supposed to get my act together?"

Why are people so intense about resumes? Bringing up the subject is almost as likely to heat up a discussion as mentioning religion or politics, yet resumes don't have nearly the significance of the other two subjects. Or do they?

Have you noticed that job seekers seem to fall into two camps: those who have absolute convictions about their resume strategy and those who constantly second-guess themselves? Why do reasonable people with good self-esteem tend to turn into overbearing control freaks or indecisive wimps when confronted with writing a resume? What is behind this Dr. Jekyll becomes Mr. Hyde/Mr. Milquetoast syndrome? Consider the following:

☆ Finding the ideal job can become a crusade instead of a research project if job seekers believe a career is crucial to personal identity. When a resume serves as an initial introduction to a potential employer, its author may endow it with far more importance than it really deserves. In this kind of self-imposed pressure-cooker situation, job seekers may protect themselves by locking on to one approach and denying all others, or trap themselves in a web of indecision to avoid making a wrong choice.

☆ Therapists say the American culture has generated a "stroke-deprived economy" by teaching us not to give, receive or ask for positive feedback. Unfortunately, resumes require us to break the rules and brag about ourselves. Faced with the distasteful prospect of committing a social taboo, we often respond with classic avoidance behavior.

☆ Because we don't learn about resumes as part of our formal or informal education, we feel a little lost when forced to write one. Consider how you would react to someone asking you to parallel park an 18-wheeler. You know it can be done, because you've seen other people pull it off who are no more intelligent than you. Yet because you have had no exposure to the technique, the process takes on an unnerving mystique. With a few lessons and a little practice, you could whip that sucker into a loading dock as well as the next guy, but for the moment, you can't trust yourself to do it without causing major damage. From this perspective, resumes and really big trucks have a lot in common.

☆ Going to the library or bookstore and looking through the resume section can be a baffling experience. Every expert seems to have a different opinion of what employers want. Chances are that the more information you gather, the more confused you'll become. It's easy to get frustrated and angry when answers aren't black and write when you desperately want them to be. Unfortunately, resumes are both an art and a science. Every expert gives good advice based on personal opinion and experience. Yet only you can determine which suggestions fit your specific situation. If you're a novice at selling yourself to potential employers, figuring out which recommendations make the most sense can be very difficult.

. . . And Its Cure

You can rise above the resume fray and confidently make your own decisions by keeping a few key facts in mind:

☆ Should you find yourself looking upon a resume as your only lifeline to employment, lighten up. It's just one tool in your job search arsenal.

☆ Remind yourself that bragging is a healthy and admirable activity when you're selling yourself to a new employer. She wants to know what you can do for her and she needs to be certain that her number one candidate is an outstanding performer. Telling her about your accomplishments helps her to justify the decision to hire you.

☆ Target each resume for a particular job. If you determine what a specific employer wants, then select past achievements that correlate with the requirements of his opening, you can be confident your resume will capture his attention and get you an interview.

☆ Ask for advice if you need it. Read resume books, talk to friends and fellow job seekers or visit a career counselor. Just don't allow any of these resources to usurp your power to choose what should be in your resume. People can determine what's right for them by trusting their instincts. There's nothing magic about writing a good resume. As long as you address both your needs and the needs of your potential employer, you'll be fine.

Reasons for Writing Resumes

Now that we have dealt with the emotion surrounding resumes, let's take a look at the reasons for writing them. As everyone knows, a resume is the usual vehicle for responding to an ad. Employers who advertise for candidates to fill a position want to screen potential employees before they OK them for interviews. Reviewing applicants' resumes is an excellent way to sort out the real contenders from those whose qualifications match poorly. To survive the winnowing process, your resume must speak concisely and directly to the needs of the recruiter. It must entice him to get to know you better.

Resumes serve a similar purpose at executive search firms. Sending a resume to a headhunter notifies her of your interest in being considered for search assignments on which she's working. To capture her attention, you must discuss your most important accomplishments in a format she will appreciate. Search firms don't work for you, so to be considered as a viable candidate, you must meet their strongest expectations.

You can also use a resume for a limited direct mail campaign to employers who particularly interest you. After identifying each company's likely requirements for potential employees, tailor your resume to highlight relevant achievements. By addressing specific needs, you should pique a recruiter's curiosity sufficiently for him to grant you an interview.

Resumes can also remind a potential employer of ways that your background might be useful. Talking to company representatives informally can help you to learn valuable facts about what the firm wants in an ideal associate. Then, if your experience seems to be a good match, you can send a resume targeting its needs. This may lead to your filling a current opening or creating a new position for yourself.

When used properly, this approach puts you miles ahead of competitors who rely on paper versus personal communication, and assumptions instead of facts about the employer's preferences.

Writing a resume also is great mental exercise before an interview. When meeting hiring managers, you should have two main goals:

1. Convincing your interviewer that you are the best candidate for the job.
2. Ascertaining if the position and the company are right for you.

Because a resume distills the achievements most relevant to the job you seek, organizing and writing this sales document requires you to consider carefully what you have to offer a particular employer. As your brain processes and refines this information, it wears comfortable little paths to its data storage centers. Then, when you need to cite your accomplishments in an interview, the information will come to you in a flash because your brain has been programmed to retrieve it easily.

What's another name for an unemployed person? A consultant. But if you're genuinely operating a consulting business, you'll probably need a resume to reinforce your credibility. Potential customers are just as concerned about your background and expertise as potential employers. They want to know you deserve to be called an expert and aren't using the title "Consultant" because you have delusions of grandeur.

Having a resume also is helpful if you work for a company that provides products or service to clients. Even if you represent one of the Big Six or a prestigious department in your corporation, you should be prepared to explain on paper why your credentials are more suited to an assignment than a competitor's. Institutions don't have the clout and credibility they once had. As the power and influence of the individual gains importance, potential users of your talents and expertise will demand to know more about you—regardless of the organization you represent.

Finally, you need a resume if you're contemplating a job change within your organization.

While resumes are valuable tools in your job search, they'll never substitute for person-to-person contact. Use them effectively to get your foot in the door, remind an employer why you should be hired, prepare for an interview or reinforce your credibility, but never assume a resume can take the place of building mutual rapport. Since the dawn of history (and probably even before that), people have done business together because they like and trust each other. This is an irrevocable trait of human nature. Use it to your advantage.

A Note from the Author

When the *National Business Employment Weekly* asked me to author a book on resumes, I struggled with many conflicting questions: How could I put together a resource that would be different from the others already on the market? What kinds of information should I include? How should I explain the resume's role in the overall job-search process? What were the best methods for illustrating how to write good resumes? What did job seekers want to know about this subject that other books weren't telling them?

To answer these questions, I read many resume books available from the library and local bookstores, then asked clients and colleagues what they expected to find in the ultimate resume guide. Here's what I discovered.

People have a number of misconceptions about resumes, especially concerning their role in a typical job search. Without discounting the importance of resumes, I wanted to dispel the myth that they're the "Open Sesame" to a new career. I chose to make my point by telling the saga of Larry and Joe and giving the resume quiz in Chapter 1.

As with any worthwhile project, preparing to put together a resume may take as long or longer than actually writing it. So often, job seekers become frustrated because they lack key items of information. Unless they first determine their marketable expertise and who's interested in buying it, they'll miss the mark in developing a truly effective written sales tool. Chapter 2 outlines how to identify your most relevant skills and accomplishments and learn from an employer how you can specifically benefit his organization.

As I looked through the books currently available on resumes, I noticed that they generally seemed to follow a prescribed format that leaves little room for individuality. Because an outstanding resume must be a personal expression of who you are, I didn't want this book to take a cookie-cutter or fill-in-the-blank approach. I especially didn't want, say, a financial planner to be able to turn to a financial planning resume, delete the name and address, put in her own and think her resume work was complete. So I used two techniques to encourage independent thinking:

1. The resumes in this book belong to real people from throughout the United States. While these examples represent and reinforce the principles I've

suggested, they depict a variety of approaches for putting together an attention-getting document.

2. To help you create a unique product that gets results, I have provided lots of ideas and examples to guide you through the process. The old cliche, "If you give a person a fish, he will eat today, but if you teach him how to fish, he will never go hungry," represents the philosophy behind this book. If you use the system I recommend instead of just cloning an example, you'll never have to grapple with the uncertainty of writing a resume, no matter what career you're in.

One client gave me some particularly valuable advice when she suggested that I include some "before" and "after" examples that were actually quite good in the "before" stage but even better in the "after" version. She said, "Don't insult your readers' intelligence by offering truly terrible 'befores.' Make people think about why seemingly subtle improvements spell the difference between a resume that gets an interview and one that doesn't." You will find before-and-after examples in most of the chapters.

A veteran career planner who had also been a successful engineer, minister and trainer, admonished me to tell the stories behind the resumes. He said, "Wouldn't it be wonderful for your readers to hear how people in similar circumstances have changed their lives and moved on to positions and organizations that use their best skills and appreciate their contributions?" I hope you'll enjoy the true stories in this book as much as I have.

If you've read many resume guides, you've probably noticed that resume examples are usually categorized by type of career or industry. Yet I've found that accountants, engineers and other pros who want to remain in their fields have less trouble putting together resumes than those making major career or lifestyle changes. The professionals most in need of a map are the ones who are charting new territory. Consequently, I've targeted four groups of adventurers for my specialized resume categories: first-time job seekers, homemakers returning to the workforce, career changers and seasoned professionals who've been with one company for a long time. If you aren't in one of these groups, however, don't feel neglected. The other examples purposely encompass a broad spectrum of careers. It's likely your vocation is among them.

Finally, I received much feedback about the need for a system to keep track of the voluminous amounts of information and paperwork generated during a typical job search. Chapter 14 deals with this issue. If you're the kind of person who despises organizing things, take some of my suggestions. However, if you love devising the most efficient method for creating order out of chaos, have at it and send me your ideas. I'm not too proud to use them (and give you the credit) in our next edition.

So that's how this book evolved. It came together much like a typical job search. It had its ups and downs, quick inspirations and frustrating obstacles, but I had an unyielding goal throughout. It took about six months of continuing effort supported by my editors, colleagues, friends, clients and family. Now that the book is done, you and other job seekers will be its final judge. Let me know what you think.

"I'm going to level with you, Stan . . . your resume is a lemon."

1

What a Resume Can and Can't Do for You

L arry woke up full of anticipation. Today, he was to begin his career as Chief Financial Officer for Acme Software Systems, a position ideally suited to his background and skills. In the past four months, Larry had pursued his job search full time, networking with at least 50 people, collaborating with headhunters, answering ads in the *National Business Employment Weekly* and his local newspaper, mounting a targeted direct mail campaign and following up on potential leads. To stay balanced, he also scheduled time to relax, play ball with his daughter, and work off that extra 10 pounds he'd been wanting to shed for the past two years.

He's both enthusiastic and a little nervous about moving into a challenging position where he will be working with a team that fits him like a glove. While the past few months have had their ups and downs, Larry knows his job search approach produces results. Should he ever need to use it again, he's confident his winning formula will find him a great match.

Meanwhile, across town, Joe looks at the clock and notices it's already 9:30 A.M. He sighs, stares at the ceiling, and tries to convince himself to get out of bed and face another day unemployed. After six months of effort, Joe doesn't feel any closer to finding work than he did when he began looking for a job. In fact, when he was laid off, he was a lot more confident about moving easily into another mid-management position than he is today. With his seemingly marketable experience, excellent reviews, sterling references, and dynamite resume that took days to perfect, he can't help wondering, "Where did I go wrong?"

Joe's problems stem from a combination of erroneous assumptions and macho attitudes. He's made a series of mistakes that have sabotaged his opportunities and heightened his depression. Unless he changes his approach, he'll spend many more mornings under the covers pondering his fate.

Let's take a look at Joe's job search versus Larry's. The differences should speak for themselves.

To Whom It May Concern

After he was laid off, Joe worked to perfect his resume like a man possessed. He carefully constructed a chronological listing of his job responsibilities to impress even the fussiest employer. He consulted his thesaurus, fine-tuning every phrase for maximum impact. After days of exhaustive labor, he pronounced his masterpiece complete and ready to catapult him into any position a contact, executive search firm, ad or direct mail campaign might offer. He honestly believed this resume was one of his life's proudest achievements.

Having produced the perfect resume and an equally perfect cover letter, Joe spent several hundred dollars on typesetting and laser printing to make hundreds of perfect copies at a local graphics firm.

While Joe put a lot of effort into his resume, he confined his networking effort to just a few friends and relatives. He was embarrassed about being laid off, so he didn't want to broadcast his unfortunate situation to people who respected him, or put his friends in an awkward position by asking for their help.

Instead he decided to make extensive use of executive search firms. In fact, he was really enthusiastic about other people's marketing him to potential corporations. To get names of qualified headhunters, he looked up Employment Recruiters and Executive Search Consultants in the yellow pages and sent all but the specialized ones his all-purpose resume and cover letter addressed: To Whom It May Concern. Then he waited for them to call.

Like many job seekers, Joe spent most of his job search pouring over want ads in his local newspaper, *National Business Employment Weekly,* and major dailies in other cities where he was willing to relocate. He responded to every ad remotely similar to his experience, assuming that at least a few would bear fruit.

Joe targeted companies in his industry as well. He went to the library and found a list of the top 250 software firms in the United States, and sent the human resources department at each company an identical resume and cover letter with a note asking them to call him if they wanted more information.

Joe, confident in the knowledge he had "papered the world" with his resume, decreased his job search efforts and eagerly anticipated an avalanche of calls and letters from prospective employers. Much to his surprise and frustration, 400 resumes generated six responses and one job offer he didn't want.

Joe started his job search believing his experience would be marketable in any number of places. In a burst of frenzied activity, he sent hundreds of unsolicited resumes to search firms and companies, answered many want ads, and did a little networking with friends. By the second month, when he began receiving rejection letters, he experienced the sinking feeling his job search would be more difficult than expected. In fact, the task began to loom larger and larger until Joe felt crushed by its weight and scope. Was he really as good as he thought? Would he ever find another job? Negative expectations overwhelmed him, crowding out all the positive feelings he had about himself, and usurping the time and effort he should have been spending looking for a job.

Every time he picked up the want ads and saw nothing worthwhile; every time he read about another layoff; and every time receipt of his resume went unacknowledged, he sank deeper into despair. Yet he did nothing to seek support from his family, friends and community because he was embarrassed and afraid.

Why didn't Joe talk to his minister, a career counselor or a therapist? Pride. Strong men don't need help. They solve their own problems.

I'm Available

When he started his job search, the first thing Larry did was list contacts who might be able to help him find a new position. Then he systematically met with each of them to explore a new career.

Recognizing that 80 to 90 percent of jobs are filled through networking, he talked extensively with potential employers. When he uncovered an opportunity, he constructed a resume to parallel the position's requirements and sent it along with a "Thank you for the appointment" note. As you might imagine, Larry eventually developed quite a stack of resume variations. But the thought and effort he put into them paid major dividends by showing potential employers how his background uniquely fit their particular needs.

While Larry knew the highest percentages of job seekers found positions through networking, he recognized that executive search firms, ads, and targeted resume campaigns sometimes yield results as well. Consequently, he researched headhunters and selected several who specialized in his field. Before he left his position at Snyder Systems, he talked to each of them to find out what they prefer in a resume and how they match candidates to search assignments. Then, focusing on his most relevant experience, he followed each firm's favored format and sent a copy of his resume to be edited, revised and resubmitted.

Perusing his local paper and *National Business Employment Weekly* ads, he selected a few that required his particular combination of skills and experience. He carefully tailored his resume to parallel what each ad requested by rearranging the priority of his accomplishments, altering jargonal phrases, highlighting key personality traits, and even changing his objective to match the position, title and company name. He became a dedicated stickler for detail. Friends in human resources positions had forewarned him, "Resumes are screening tools. Even one 'off the mark' element can be the kiss of death."

Instead of beginning his cover letter with the usual, "I am sending my resume in response to your ad for a CFO," he did some library research that enabled him to focus his first paragraph on why the company interested him. Having attracted the attention of the human resources department with this unique approach, Larry summarized his most relevant experiences in his second paragraph. At the end of the letter, he promised a follow-up call to answer any immediate questions and discuss the mutual benefit of scheduling an initial interview. Of course, he addressed the letter to a specific person, even if it required a little sleuthing to discover the name, while also sending a copy to the CEO when possible.

To launch his very selective direct mail campaign, Larry spent several days at the library researching companies to determine his best corporate candidates. He looked for those whose philosophy, growth, organization, and products or services intrigued him. As he read annual reports and trade journal articles, he searched for specific needs or niches he might uniquely fill. After having tailored his cover letters and resumes, he sent them to the targeted CEOs most likely to hire him, then followed up on the phone to find out if a get-acquainted interview would be worthwhile.

By carefully pursuing chosen markets through networking, search firms, ads and direct mail, Larry maximized his chances for generating serious responses. By the time his job search ended, he had produced 20 inquiries, 10 initial interviews, 6 second interviews and 4 job offers, all of which were good matches for his background and interests.

I'm OK

Larry knew his job search would be a roller coaster of "king of the hill" highs and "crawl under a snake with a high hat on" lows. Consequently, he built a variety of activities into his days to keep himself on an even keel.

While he pursued a new job five days a week, he didn't obsess about it. As a recovering workaholic, he didn't want to backslide by concentrating on his job search every waking hour. He knew actively seeking a balance of work, fun and learning was a healthy approach whether he was employed or not. And he was hoping if he practiced his new lifestyle during his job search, he would be more likely to maintain it when he returned to work.

A Resume Doesn't a Job Search Make

Larry's and Joe's stories illustrate that a perfect resume doesn't produce a satisfying career. Unless your job search strategy combines a savvy resume with lots of networking, targeted marketing, persistent follow-up and psychological support, you, too, may find yourself depressed, unemployed and wondering what went wrong.

A Resume Quiz

The saga of Larry and Joe has alluded to a number of activities and attitudes involving resumes. Now that you have read it, here's a quiz to test your resume acumen. Don't worry if you don't answer all the questions correctly. If you were an expert, you would be writing this book, not reading it (the correct answers follow the quiz):

1. Any well-planned job search begins with a great resume. T or F (True or False)?
2. When putting together a cover letter and resume for an ad, you:
   A. Tailor both the letter and the resume.
   B. Send a generic letter and resume.
   C. Tailor the cover letter, not the resume.
3. Armed with a good resume, a headhunter has all he needs to market you to a variety of potential employers. T or F?
4. A resume is your most important job search tool. T or F?

5. Potential employers would rather hire an employed person than someone without a job. T or F?

6. The research you conduct to formulate your resume is also an important key to preparing for an employment interview. T or F?

7. Employers consider your resume follow-up a waste of their time. T or F?

8. You can expect to get a reply from everyone to whom you send a resume. T or F?

9. There is one resume format most employers prefer. T or F?

10. The most effective job search activity is:

   A. Answering ads.

   B. Networking with follow-up.

   C. Using a search firm.

   D. Mounting a direct mail campaign.

11. The best way to begin a cover letter is with a unique reason for your interest in the company and available position. T or F?

12. Looking for a job is much harder than filling an opening, because the employer is always in the driver's seat. T or F?

13. In real estate, the three keys to success are location, location, and location. In writing resumes, it's tailoring, tailoring, tailoring. T or F?

14. Use the name of the person and company to whom you are sending your resume in cover letters, even if it takes some sleuthing to discover it. T or F?

15. With the perfect resume, you will be able to leap tall buildings in a single bound, catch bullets in your teeth, and land a position that pays $500K, plus stock options. T or F?

1. **False.** Despite conventional wisdom, you do not want to start your job search with a major resume effort. To do this puts the cart before the horse. A resume is really a kind of ad or brochure. Before developing an ad campaign, an advertising agency carefully targets its market and defines its customers' needs and priorities. Only after identifying these factors, does the copywriter describe features and benefits most useful to the targeted market. In your case, you are the product. You bear the responsibility of selling your most important experiences and attributes to potential employers on a person-to-person basis. If you write your resume before you have found out what they need, you are missing an opportunity to present your best case.

2. A. Tailor both the resume and cover letter. How many times have you heard people say they customize their cover letter, but send the same resume to everyone? Usually they are very proud of themselves for doing this, as many job seekers send one form letter and resume to everyone. Unfortunately, when a resume is competing with 200 to 400 others, it has to stand out from the crowd. Recruiters don't have time to separate the "diamonds from the dirt" in the 30 to 60 seconds they spend skimming for relevant experience. It is the candidate's responsibility to sort the valuable stuff from the extraneous, using only 20-carat material to land an interview.

3. False. Executive search firms need a good resume from you, but they also must have a search assignment that matches your background before they can be of service. Headhunters do not market you. They find the best candidates for client job openings. Their clients are companies that pay their fee or retainer. Don't expect a headhunter to make you her number one marketing project. Conducting your search campaign isn't her job, it's yours.

4. False. A resume is an important tool, but it can't get you a job. Only people can do that. If you want your job search to be successful, concentrate on people and prepare your resume to suit their needs.

5. False. It used to be true that firms preferred to hire employed people because only the deadwood were let go from a company. However, in the past several years, corporate mergers and acquisitions, hostile takeovers, and right-sizings have put many highly qualified professionals on the street through no fault of their own. Prospective employers are aware of this trend. If you maintain your self-confidence and tell a potential employer what you can do for him, he will consider another firm's loss his gain.

6. True. Resume search is important for the job interview, too. Most of us are more comfortable moving into unfamiliar territory if we have a map of the terrain. When you have researched an individual company to tailor your resume, you know a great deal about its products—services, mission, philosophy, revenues, and so forth. This information can be very valuable in preparing good questions and answers for initial and subsequent interviews. Employers like candidates who are savvy enough to do some homework before their first meeting.

In customizing your resume, you are pursuing two objectives simultaneously: You are creating a powerful written sales tool, and you are developing a verbal testament about why a specific employer should hire you. If you think of your resume-writing process as the best preparation for a rigorous interview session, you will be more likely to give it the time it deserves.

7. **False.** Employers don't consider your resume follow-up a waste of their time. While there will always be potential employers who are firm believers in the "don't call us, we'll call you" approach, most recruiters admire candidates who make an effort to follow up on their resumes. Follow-up shows both initiative and persistence, traits good managers love, especially in individuals who are applying for positions with major responsibilities. Don't worry about seeming too enthusiastic. Company representatives enjoy being pursued. It massages their egos and reminds them their company is worth courting.

8. **False.** Replying to all resumes would be the polite thing to do, but often it simply isn't practical. If a company receives 200 responses for an ad, or experiences a continual deluge of unsolicited resumes, it would spend an inordinate amount of time sending acknowledgments. If you really want a receipt for your resume, send a stamped, self-addressed postcard asking for one. If you make it easy, the human resources department will comply.

9. **False.** There is no universally preferred format. Many job seekers spend days perfecting their resumes, agonizing over whether to use a chronological format or a functional one. This question may be akin to figuring how many angels will fit on the head of a pin. There is no one perfect resume to suit every employer's needs. But there is a perfect resume for a specific opportunity. If you are going to focus on perfection, do it on an individual, rather than a global basis.

10. **B.** Networking with follow-up is the most effective. The key to a successful job search is contacts. Most people can sell themselves better in person than on paper. While the tailored resumes you send to search firms, ads and direct mail targets are important and deserve your attention, they will never possess the power of a good relationship.

11. **True.** Just about every cover letter sent in response to an ad begins in the following style, "To Whom It May Concern: This letter is in response to your ad in the *National Business Employment Weekly* for . . ." Rather uninspiring, isn't it? Is it any wonder the few individuals who research a company, then use the information to formulate their cover letter's first paragraph, have a tremendous advantage over their complacent competitors? In the resume derby, everything you do to distinguish yourself moves you another length ahead of the pack.

12. **False.** Have you ever tried to hire a new employee? While looking for a job is tough, finding a good employee is no picnic either. Picture yourself

as the CEO of a small to midsize company looking for a new CFO. After carefully constructing your ad, you wade through scores of resumes, schedule and conduct several rounds of interviews, screen the princes from the frogs, and hope when you choose the best candidate, he will say yes. For a busy executive, this can be a long, expensive, and nerve-racking process with no guarantee of a positive result.

13. **True.** Tailor, tailor, tailor.

14. **True.** People and companies like to see their names in print, especially if it took some effort to find them. Chapters 2 and 5 include tips to help you find the real addressee even when the person is trying to be incognito.

15. **Unfortunately, false, superexec.** However, a great resume can get you invited to the penthouse, where your masterful interviewing techniques will lead to a great opportunity complete with a substantial raise and a covered parking spot with your name on it.

2

Getting Organized

Before you make your first networking call or circle any ads in the newspaper, prepare an office at home or at an outplacement facility to maximize your productivity and keep frustration to a minimum.

If you haven't already acquainted yourself with the power and ease of desktop publishing, do it now. With a current word-processing package and a PC, you can produce a variety of professional looking, tailored resumes and cover letters without having to retype each version or pay an expensive resume service. And while the computer is saving you time, money and aggravation on your resumes, it can also store your contact and company data, keep your weekly calendar, monitor your cash flow, remind you to follow up on resumes and appointments and even play a game with you if you need a little diversion.

If you don't have a computer or can't gain easy access to one through a friend, college lab, or outplacement center, copy businesses such as Kinko's rent them by the hour. You might also check the cost of having your resumes and cover letters typed by personnel at an executive office service, especially if you are contracting with them to receive your mail and answer your calls during the day.

Aside from a computer, you'll need a few other important resources to create professional resumes. A laser or ink jet printer is one of them. While a dot matrix printer may be perfectly presentable for your son's sixth-grade science project, its product will not serve you well in a competitive job market. If you don't have a good printer or the funds to buy one, take your resume disk to a local print shop where it will be translated into a hard copy for you.

If you have read any older resume books, you have probably noticed how outdated the typefaces look. With the advent of desktop publishing, your little computer can produce beautiful documents from software that contain a variety of type sizes, italics, bold lettering and other techniques previously seen only in expensive documents. Before you type your resume, be sure you have at least one modern font available which reflects your personality. When your resume is competing with 200 others, you don't want it to be eliminated because it looks as if you wrote it wearing a leisure suit.

You should order some fine-quality stationery for your cover letters and resumes. Quality paper has a high rag content and a watermark you can see if you hold it up to the light. There isn't any one color preferred over others. So you can assert your independence and select something in the white, cream, light blue, or gray color family without concern about being incorrect.

You may want to have your name, address, and phone number printed on your letterhead, and your name and address on the envelopes. While it isn't necessary to do this, it can save you some time, and it has a finished quality that lends an added touch of distinction.

Aside from a computer, printer, diskholder and stationery, you will want to stock your work space with the following important tools:

- ☆ *Stamps*—both first and third class varieties—in case you need to send some heavier packages.
- ☆ A *rolodex*—manual or computerized—for quick reference to contact and company names, addresses and phone numbers.
- ☆ A *wall or desk calendar* for scheduling blocks of time for research, phone calls, resumes and cover letters, thank-you notes, brainstorming, reading

ads, articles and books, interviews, notes on appointments, and appropriate follow-up strategies.

☆ A *system* for keeping track of your job search activities and the follow-up needed for each.

☆ A *dictionary or thesaurus* for checking spelling and finding just the right word whenever you need it.

Laying Your Resume Foundation

Writing a great resume is a lot like painting a house. Before you apply the paint, you have to buy the right materials, assemble them, and prepare your surface. If you neglect these initial steps, your final product will probably fall short of your standards. Taking a systematic approach may seem to require more time at the outset, but sticking to it will save you a lot of frustrated effort and produce superior results.

Accomplishments History

Before writing one word of your resume, put together an accomplishments history, including your most significant achievements from work, hobbies, volunteer projects, school, extracurricular activities, travel, and other life experiences you feel are worth noting. Doing this is essential to preparing a good resume, and it's a wonderful boost for the bruised ego commonly found in job seekers.

For each of your chosen accomplishments, create a list of chronological activities, transferable and specialized skills, and results. Mention names of clients, companies, participants, states, clubs, institutions, and individuals that would impress a potential employer. Quantify where applicable. Some examples of relevant statistics might include sales volume, percentage increase in revenue, inventory turns, money saved, percentage of shrinkage decrease or worker hours saved. You can also give a better idea of the scope of your job or project by quantifying the number of people you supervise, coordinate, collaborate with or serve as customers.

Be creative and inclusive in describing what you've done. This is not the appropriate time for modesty. You might want to involve your spouse or a friend in this process. Often they remember your accomplishments better than you do, and they can encourage you to give yourself credit for efforts you might dismiss as trivial. The following are some examples of achievements to help get your brainstorming started:

☆ Designing a brochure, poster or newsletter.

☆ Mediating a dispute between two parties.

☆ Determining the political realities in choosing a course of action.

☆ Selling a product, service or decision to senior executives or clients.

☆ Developing, promoting and teaching in-house training programs.

☆ Putting together a yearly project or budget.

☆ Investigating the options for installing a new system.

☆ Supervising and mentoring professional or blue-collar workers.

☆ Inventing a new product or service.

☆ Speaking to large or small groups or chairing committee meetings.

☆ Writing and editing an employee or product documentation manual.

☆ Spearheading organizational change.

☆ Working on a team to design a mission statement and policies.

☆ Fixing a product design problem.

☆ Establishing rapport with people whose perspectives are different from yours.

☆ Opening a new facility.

☆ Recruiting and interviewing potential employees.

☆ Planning an advertising or public relations campaign.

☆ Using your imagination to solve a pressing or recurring problem.

☆ Testing a hypothesis to determine if your hunch is correct.

☆ Implementing a total quality program.

☆ Acting quickly and decisively to avert a crisis or take advantage of an opportunity.

☆ Prioritizing, juggling a variety of tasks.

☆ Inspiring people to do difficult things.

☆ Coaching a soccer team.

☆ Planning and hosting a 25th-anniversary party.

☆ Traveling to a new and exotic place.

☆ Building and flying a model airplane.

☆ Renovating and managing rental houses.

☆ Doing your own income tax return.

☆ Serving as an officer for a nonprofit agency.

☆ Managing your own portfolio.

☆ Losing 25 pounds and maintaining your new weight.

☆ Adding a gameroom to the house.

Once you've made a list of your accomplishments, give each of them its own sheet of paper and write about the step-by-step process you used to make it successful. The following is an example of a typical achievement:

LARRY'S NUMBER ONE ACCOMPLISHMENT

My most significant accomplishment as chief financial and administrative officer was starting an Investor Relations program from scratch after my company went public in 1989. For the first year, I handled IR personally, but then recognized we needed a much more proactive program than I was able to provide using 25 percent of my available time. Basically, I was just responding to securities analysts' questions and was not able to court new analysts or visit existing shareholders.

In 1991, I hired a top-notch IR VP from a giant competitor. He spent about 75 percent of his first year traveling. He had phone conversations with 100 analysts and face-to-face meetings with another 115 of the most important analysts or potential investors. Our CEO, the IR VP and I made formal slide presentations to 10 industry analyst meetings. Our shareholder list improved from 5 percent retail (individual stockholders as opposed to institutions who owned stock) to 25 percent, and we increased the number of analysts who wrote reports on our company from 2 to 10.

The experience utilized several of my skills/attributes that are important to me:

1. My ability to find and motivate good people—everyone thought very highly of our IR VP, and he worked tirelessly during the time he was with us.

2. My credibility—we were honest and forthright with analysts and they thanked us for it.

3. My presentation skills—I was able to bring to the process all the key ingredients in effective presentations:
    • Understanding the important aspects of the business.
    • Understanding what the audience wants to know about the company.
    • Good charts and written materials.
    • Good verbal skills.

Once you have written your accomplishments, put them on a skills summary sheet. Doing this will help you select action verbs and phrases to describe your most marketable activities to potential employers. The functional and transferable skills inventory starting on page 25 shows how Larry has identified the functional skills he used to achieve his IR department goal.

While most people think they know the skills they use on a regular basis, they often neglect to identify some of their most important competencies, especially those that are inborn and come naturally. Yet these functional skills are primary keys to an individual's effectiveness and are usually essential ingredients to a satisfying position.

Your Functional and Transferable Skills Inventory

Creating a resume without having a solid grasp of the skills you use best (and enjoy most) is an impossible task. To gain a better understanding of your key abilities and how they might transfer to new functional areas, complete a skills inventory worksheet like the following sample, which documents Larry's IR experience.

FUNCTIONAL AND TRANSFERABLE SKILLS INVENTORY

DIRECTIONS:

☆ Choose seven experiences from any time (current, childhood, teen years, college, etc., 5-10-20 years ago, etc.) and any area (work, family, school, volunteer work, hobbies, special projects, relationships, etc.) of your life using two criteria:

1. They were satisfying.

2. You enjoyed their *process* as well as their result.

☆ Write a paragraph or outline giving a step-by-step account of each one.

☆ Think about why you chose these seven experiences and what you particularly enjoyed about them.

☆ On this skills exercise, put the title of your first experience at the top of Column 1 Then—keeping in mind its step-by-step process–look at each box of transferable skills. If you used one or more of the skills in a box, put a check in Column 1. If you enjoyed using the skill(s), make a second check (in the same box).

☆ As you work through Column 1, you will find that some skills have no checks because you didn't use them in your experience. Some will have one check: You used them but they weren't enjoyable. Others will have two checks: You had fun applying them.

☆ After completing Column 1, use the same procedure for your other six experiences.

☆ Your completed exercise will give an excellent picture of your transferable skills, where they cluster, and which ones are most satisfying.

Experiences	IR. Program	1	2	3	4	5	6	7
I. THE SOCIAL THEME (People and Idea Skills)								
A. Written Communication Skills								
Love of reading voraciously or rapidly. Love of printed things.								
Comparing. Editing effectively.		✓✓						
Publishing imaginatively.								
Explicit, concise writing. Keeping superior minutes of meetings.		✓✓						
Uncommonly warm letter composition.		✓✓						
Flair for writing reports. Skilled in speechwriting.								
B. Verbal Communication Skills								
Effective verbal communication. Expressing self very well. Making a point and cogently expressing a position.		✓✓						
Encouraging communication and participation.		✓✓						
Thinking quickly on one's feet.		✓						
Translating. Verbal skills in foreign languages. Teaching languages. Adept at translating jargon into relevant and meaningful terms to diverse audiences or readers.		✓✓						

	IR. Program						
	1	2	3	4	5	6	7
Summarizing. Reporting on conversations or meetings accurately.							
Informing, enlightening, explaining, instructing, defining.	✓✓						
Developing rapport and trust.	✓✓						
Adept at two-way dialogue. Ability to hear and answer questions perceptively. Accepting differing opinions. Helping others express their views.	✓✓						
Listening intently and accurately. Good at listening and conveying awareness.	✓✓						
Dealing with many different kinds of people. Talks easily with all kinds of people.							
C. Instructing, Guiding, Mentoring Skills							
Fostering stimulating learning environment. Creating an atmosphere of acceptance. Patient teaching. Instills love of the subject. Conveys tremendous enthusiasm.							
Adept at inventing illustrations for principles or ideas. Adept at using visual communications.	✓✓						
Coaching, advising, aiding people in making decisions.	✓✓						
Consulting.							
Mentoring and facilitating personal growth and development. Helping people make their own discoveries in knowledge, ideas or insights. Empowering.							
Clarifying goals and values of others. Puts things in perspective.	✓✓						
Fostering creativity in others. Showing others how to use resources.							
Group facilitating. Discussion group leadership. Group dynamics.							
Training. Designing educational events. Organizing and administering in-house training programs.							
D. Serving/Helping/Human Relations Skills							
Relating well in dealing with the public/public relations.	✓✓						
Helping and serving. Referring (people). Customer relations and services.							

	IR. Program						
	1	2	3	4	5	6	7
Sensitivity to others. Interested in/manifesting keen ability to relate to people. Adept at treating people fairly. Consistently communicates warmth to people. Conveying understanding, patience and fairness.							
Perceptive in identifying and assessing the potential of others. Recognizes and appreciates the skills of others.							
Remembering people and their preferences.							
Keen ability to put self in someone else's shoes. Empathy. Instinctively understands others feelings.							
Tact, diplomacy and discretion.	✓✓						
Caring for. Watching over. Nurturing.							
Administering a household.							
Shaping and influencing the atmosphere of a particular place. Providing comfortable, natural, and pleasant surroundings.	✓✓						
Warmly sensitive and responsive to people's feelings and needs in social or other situation. Anticipating people's needs.	✓✓						
Working well on a team. Has fun while working and makes it fun for others. Collaborating with colleagues skillfully. Treating others as equals without regard to education, authority or position. Motivates fellow workers. Expresses appreciation faithfully. Ready willingness to share credit with others.	✓✓						
Refusing to put people into slots or categories. Ability to relate to people with different value systems.	✓						
Taking human failings/limitations into account. Dealing patiently and sympathetically with difficult people. Handles prima donnas tactfully and effectively. Works well in hostile environment.	✓						
Nursing. Skillful therapeutic abilities.							
Gifted at helping people with their personal problems. Raises people's self-esteem. Understands human motivations, relationships and needs. Aware of people's need for supportive community. Aids people with their total life adjustment. Counseling.							

	IR. Program						
	1	2	3	4	5	6	7
Unusual ability to represent others. Expert in liaison roles. Ombudsmanship.	✓✓						
II. THE ENTERPRISING THEME (People, Idea and System Skills)							
A. Influencing/Persuading Skills							
Helping people identify their own intelligent self-interest.	✓✓						
Persuading. Influencing the attitudes or ideas of others.	✓✓						
Promoting. Face-to-face selling of tangibles/intangibles. Selling ideas or products without tearing down competing ideas or products. Selling an idea, program or course of action to decision makers.	✓✓						
Making and using contacts effectively. Resource broker.	✓✓						
Developing targets/building markets for ideas or products.	✓✓						
Raising money. Arranging financing.	✓✓						
Getting diverse groups to work together. Wins friends easily from among diverse or even opposing groups or factions.							
Adept at conflict management.							
Arbitrating/mediating between contending parties or groups. Negotiating to come jointly to decisions. Bargaining. Crisis intervention. Reconciling.							
Renegotiating. Obtaining agreement on policies, after the fact.							
Recruiting talent or leadership. Attracting skilled, competent, creative people.	✓✓						
Motivating others. Mobilizing. Stimulating people to effective action.	✓✓						
Leading others. Inspiring and leading organized groups. Impresses others with enthusiasm and charisma. Repeatedly elected to senior posts. Skilled at chairing meetings.							
Deft in directing creative talent. Skilled leadership in perceptive human relations techniques.	✓✓						
Bringing people together in cooperative efforts. Able to call in other experts/helpers as needed. Team-building. Recognizing and utilizing the skills of others.	✓✓						

	IR. Program						
	1	2	3	4	5	6	7
Directing others. Making decisions about others. Supervising others in their work. Contracting. Delegating.	✓✓						
Recognizes intergroup communications gaps. Judges people's effectiveness.	✓✓						
B. Performing Skills							
Getting up before a group. Very responsive to audiences' moods or ideas. Contributes to others' pleasure consciously. Performing.	✓						
Demonstrating. Modeling. Making presentations.	✓✓						
Showmanship. A strong theatrical sense. Poise in public appearance.	✓						
Addressing groups. Speaking ability/articulateness. Public address/public speaking/oral presentations. Lecturing. Stimulating people's enthusiasm.	✓✓						
Making people laugh. Understanding the value of the ridiculous in illuminating reality.							
Acting.							
Conducting and directing public affairs and ceremonies.							
C. Initiating/Risk-Taking Skills							
Initiating. Able to move into new situations on one's own.	✓✓						
Taking the first move in developing relationships.	✓✓						
Driving initiative. Searching for more responsibility.							
Excellent at organizing one's time. Ability to do work self-directed, without supervision.	✓✓						
Unwillingness to automatically accept the status quo. Keen perceptions of things as they could be, rather than passively accepting them as they are. Promoting and bringing about major changes. A change agent.	✓✓						
Seeing and seizing opportunities. Sees a problem and acts immediately to solve it.	✓✓						
Dealing well with the unexpected or critical. Decisive in emergencies.							

	IR. Program						
	1	2	3	4	5	6	7
Adept at confronting others with touchy or difficult personal matters.							
Entrepreneurial.							
Showing courage. Willing to take manageable risks.	✓✓						
Able to make hard decisions.							
D. Planning and Management Skills							
Planning, development. Planning on basis of lessons from past experience. A systematic approach to goal-setting.	✓✓						
Prioritizing tasks. Establishing effective priorities among competing requirements. Setting criteria or standards.	✓✓						
Policy formulation or interpretation. Creating and implementing new policies.	✓✓						
Designing projects. Program development.	✓✓						
Skilled at planning and carrying out well-run meetings, seminars or workshops.	✓✓						
Organizing. Organizational development and analysis. Planning and building. Bringing order out of chaos.	✓✓						
Scheduling, Assigning, Setting up and maintaining on-time work schedules. Coordinating operations/details. Arranging.	✓✓						
Producing. Achieving. Attaining a goal.	✓✓						
Recommending courses of action.	✓✓						
Making good use of feedback.	✓✓						
III. THE ARTISTIC THEME (Idea Skills)							
A. Intuitional and Innovating Skills							
Having imagination and the courage to use it.							
Operating well in a free, unstructured, environment. Bringing new life to traditional approaches.	✓✓						

	IR. Program						
	1	2	3	4	5	6	7
Ideophoria; continually conceiving, developing and generating ideas. Inventing. Conceptualizing.							
Improvising on the spur of the moment.							
Innovating, Perceptive, creative problem solver. Willing to experiment with new approaches.							
Love of exercising the creative mind-muscle.	✓✓						
Synthesizing perceptions. Seeing relationships between apparently unrelated factors. Integrating diverse elements into a clear, coherent whole. Ability to relate abstract ideas.	✓✓						
Deriving things from others' ideas. Improvising, Updating, Adapting.	✓✓						
Relating theory to a practical situation. Theoretical Model development.	✓✓						
Generating ideas with commercial possibilities. Seeing the commercial possibilities of abstract ideas or concepts. Creating products or services.	✓✓						
Showing foresight. Recognizing obsolescence before it occurs. Instinctively gathering resources even before the need for them is evident. Forecasting.	✓✓						
Perceiving intuitively.	✓✓						
B. Artistic Skills							
Showing strong sensitivity to, and need for, beauty in the environment. Instinctively excellent taste.							
Expressive. Exceptionally good at facial expressions used to convey thoughts without (or in addition to) words. Using voice tone and rhythm as unusually effective tool of communication. Accurately reproducing sounds (e.g., foreign languages spoken without accent).							
Good sense of humor and playfulness conveyed in person or in writing.							
Aware of the value of symbolism and deft in its use. Skilled at symbol formation (words, pictures and concepts). Visualizing concepts. Creating poetic images.							

	IR. Program						
	1	2	3	4	5	6	7
Designing and/or using audiovisual aids, photographs, visual, spatial and graphic designs. Illustrations, maps, logos.	✓✓						
Perception of forms, patterns and structures. Visualizing shapes, graphs, in the third dimension.	✓✓						
Spatial memory. Memory for design. Notice quickly (and/or remember later) most of the contents of a room. Memory for faces.							
Exceptional color discrimination.							
Designing, fashioning, shaping, redesigning things. Styling, decorating.							
Writing novels, stories, imaginative scripts, ad campaigns. Playwriting. Assisting and directing the planning, organizing, and staging of a theatrical production.							
Musical knowledge and taste. Tonal memory. Uncommon sense of rhythm. Exceedingly accurate melody recognition. Composing, making music. Dancing, singing, expert at using the body to express feelings.							
IV. THE INVESTIGATIVE THEME (Data and System Skills)							
A. Observational Learning Skills							
Highly observant of people, data and things. Keen awareness of surroundings.							
Intensely curious about people, data, things.							
Adept at scanning reports, computer printouts or other sophisticated observational systems.	✓✓						
Hearing accurately. Keen sense of smell. Excellent sense of taste.							
Detecting, discovering. A person of perpetual curiosity. Delights in new knowledge. Continually seeking to expose oneself to new experiences. Highly committed to continual personal growth and learning. Wants to know why.							
Learning from the example of others. Learns quickly.							
Alert in observing human behavior. Studying other people's behavior.	✓✓						

	IR. Program						
	1	2	3	4	5	6	7
Appraising, assessing, screening. Realistically evaluating people's needs. Accurately assessing public mood. Quickly sizing up situations and their political realities.	✓✓						
Intelligence tempered by common sense.	✓✓						
Balancing factors. Judging. Showing good judgment.	✓✓						
B. Investigating/Analyzing/Systematizing/Evaluating Skills							
Anticipating problems before they occur.	✓✓						
Recognizing need for more information before a decision can be made intelligently. Skilled at clarifying problems or situation.	✓✓						
Inspecting, examining, surveying, researching exhaustively, gathering information.	✓✓						
Interviewing people. Researching personally through investigation and interviews. Inquiring.	✓✓						
Researching resources, ways and means.	✓✓						
Dissecting, Breaking down principles into parts. Analyzing needs, values, resources, communication situations, requirements, performance specifications, etc.	✓✓						
Diagnosing. Separating "wheat from chaff." Reviewing large amounts of material and extracts essence.	✓✓						
Perceiving and defining cause-and-effect relationships. Ability to trace problems, ideas, etc. to their source.	✓✓						
Grouping, perceiving common denominators. Organizing material/information in a systematic way. Categorizing.	✓✓						
Testing an idea or hypothesis.							
Determining or figuring out, problem solving, troubleshooting.	✓✓						
Reviewing. Screening data. Critiquing, Evaluating by measurable or subjective criteria (e.g., programs, loans, papers, quizzes, work, staff, records, program bids evidence, options, qualifications, etc.).							

	IR. Program						
	1	2	3	4	5	6	7
Making decisions based on information gathered.	✓✓						
Reevaluating.							
V. THE CONVENTIONAL THEME (Data and Method Skills)							
A. Detail and Follow-Through Skills							
Following through, executing, maintaining.	✓✓						
Good at getting things done.	✓✓						
Implementing decisions. Providing support services. Applying what others have developed.							
Precise attainment of set limits, tolerances, or standards. Brings projects in on time and within budget. Skilled at making arrangements for events, processes. Responsible.	✓✓						
Expediting, dispatching. Adept at finding ways to speed up a job.							
Able to handle a great variety of tasks and responsibilities simultaneously and efficiently.	✓						
Good at getting materials. Collecting things. Purchasing. Compiling.							
Approving, validating information.	✓						
Keeping information confidential.							
Persevering.	✓						
Following detailed instructions. Keen and accurate memory for detail. Showing careful attention to, and keeping track, of details.	✓						
High tolerance of repetition and/or monotony.							
Checking, proofreading.	✓						
Systematic manipulation of data. Good at processing information. Collates/tabulates data accurately, compares current with previous data. Keeping records. Recording (kinds of data).	✓✓						
Facilitating and simplifying other people's finding things.	✓✓						

	IR. Program						
	1	2	3	4	5	6	7
Organizing written and numerical data according to a prescribed plan. Classification skills. Filing, retrieving data.	✓✓						
Clerical ability. Operating business machines and data processing machines to attain organizational and economic goals. Reproducing materials.							
B. Working with Numbers							
Numerical ability. Expert at learning and remembering numbers.	✓✓						
Counting. Taking inventory.							
Calculating, computing, arithmetic skills. Rapid manipulation of numbers. Rapid computations performed in head or on paper.	✓✓						
Managing money. Financial planning and management. Keeping financial records. Accountability.	✓✓						
Appraising, economic research and analysis, Cost Analysis, estimates, projections. Comparisons, financial/fiscal analysis and planning/programming.	✓✓						
Budget planning, preparation, justification, administration, analysis and review.	✓✓						
Extremely economical. Skilled at allocating scarce financial resources.							
Preparing financial reports.	✓✓						
Using numbers as a reasoning tool. Very sophisticated mathematical abilities. Effective at solving statistical problems.	✓✓						
VI. THE REALISTIC THEME (Thing and Method Skills)							
A. Working with Your Hands and Body							
Molding, shaping, making.							
Preparing, clearing, building, constructing, assembling, setting up, installing, laying.							
Lifting/pushing/pulling/balancing, carrying, unloading/moving delivering.							
Handling/feeling. Keen sense of touch. Finger dexterity, Manipulating things.							

	IR. Program						
	1	2	3	4	5	6	7
Precision working. Showing dexterity or speed.							
Feeding, pending.							
Controlling/operating, blasting, grinding, forging, cutting, filling, applying, pressing, binding.							
Using small or large tools, machinery. Operating vehicles or equipment.							
Fitting, adjusting, tuning, maintaining, repairing, Masters machinery against its will. Troubleshooting machine problems.							
Producing things.							
Motor/physical coordination and agility, Eye-hand-foot coordination. Walking, climbing, running.							
Skilled at sports.							
Physical recreation. Outdoor survival skills. Creating, planning, organizing outdoor activities.							
Traveling.							
Cultivating, planting and nurturing growing things. Skilled at planting/nurturing plants.							
Farming, ranching, working with animals.							

Gathering Information to Tailor Your Resume

With your accomplishments history complete, you are almost ready to begin working on your resume. So far, you have laid a foundation for describing the most important things you can offer an employer. Now you need to determine exactly what the employer wants from you. There are a variety of ways to do this by using ads, information interviews and library research.

Resume Information from Ads

Let's take a look at a typical ad in the *National Business Employment Weekly* to determine what is particularly important to the company that placed it, and how you might best respond.

E. S. Robbins, a medium-size, fast-growing plastics manufacturer is looking for a VP Sales and Marketing. If you have experience with a medium-size company on a high growth curve, be sure to include this information in your resume, and provide increasing sales figures to back it up. Since your background is similar, it will pique the recruiter's interest and entice him to continue reading for other parallels.

Robbins has multiple product lines and serves a global market. Most of its lines have been around for a while, but it also has a fast-growing new one at the forefront of its market niche. If you have experience in a worldwide market, focus on it. If you have worked with any fast-moving, cutting-edge products, this will be a key selling point for you.

The next part of the ad makes your job of interpreting what the company wants very simple. They've listed their major requirements for you. Consequently, you should address every one of the five bulleted items to have the best chance of landing an interview.

The fourth paragraph alludes to the company's corporate philosophy. It wants leaders who are team players, responsive to customer and company needs, driven by a dedication to quality and committed to the continual innovation of products. Referring to these more general, but highly important criteria in your resume will definitely win you some kudos.

Finally, the company expects you to move to Alabama if you want this position. Mentioning your willingness to relocate would be to your advantage as well.

While the preceding ad is pretty straightforward, others require some reading in between the lines. Let's take a look at one that will test your powers of observation and interpretation.

The company running this ad is a fast-growing consulting firm that wants people who will work hard, put in a good deal of overtime, travel extensively and get along with each other. It needs generalists who will look at the entire client

Strategy/Value Creation Consulting

Fast growing consulting firm seeks exceptionally bright, motivated, team-oriented individuals. Practice highly focused on assisting client companies achieve full financial and operating potential; create long-term value.

CONSULTANTS Required: Two years at leading corporate strategy consulting firm. MBA from top school. Operating experience or financial expertise a plus.

ANALYSTS Required: One year at leading corporate strategy consulting firm. Exceptional academic record. Financial modeling and computer skills.

Write to:

Cooper, McPhee & Associates, Inc.
Attn: Human Resources
70 Walnut Street, Wellesley, MA 02181
Please, no calls

operation and develop options to impact long-term results, rather than bottom line this quarter. Experience and education from leading businesses and academic institutions are very important to them.

If you want to impress their human resource professionals, be prepared to discuss high-profile projects geared to positioning your clients for long-term outcomes in organizational development, financial planning and analysis, management information systems, marketing strategies and other functions that affect the company as a whole. While specific experience in operations and finance would be useful, they are not looking for specialists, who focus only on one aspect of the business. And if your MBA is from a small, but proud regional institution, you can probably forget about this opportunity. You may have a fine education, but Harvard, Northwestern or University of Pennsylvania graduates will most certainly have the edge at this firm.

Resume Information on Companies Targeted for a Direct Mail Campaign

Along with ads, networking and executive search firms, you may want to target some potential employers for a direct mail campaign. Any direct mail expert will tell you this type of communication is very much a numbers game. The usual response rate ranges between 1 and 5 percent. Consequently, if you want 10 replies to your mailing, you will have to send out between 200 and 1,000 resumes. When you consider the time, effort and money needed to mount this size campaign, it's apparent that papering the world with your resume is an exercise in diminishing marginal utility.

If you target potential employers very carefully, however, you can do a limited mailout and receive a reasonable return on your investment. To choose your best candidates, head for the business section of your nearest large library, where you will find an overwhelming abundance of reference material. Once there, go directly to the librarian and ask for help. Believe it or not, librarians would much rather help you to find information than hide in the stacks. To facilitate their search, put together a list of demographics describing the types of employer you want to research. The company's industry, revenue, number of employees, geographical area, product or service, public or private ownership, profit or nonprofit status, years in business and contribution to the community are all attributes that might be useful.

If you can't find the librarian, or if she's busy or having a bad day, here are a few key resources that can provide data for writing cover letters and resumes designed to attract your target employers:

☆ *The Infotrac System.* This database contains the same information as the *Readers' Guide to Periodical Literature.* It has articles listed by company name, the author's name, and subject area from periodicals published in the past three years. If you want to access older material, you will have to use the *Readers' Guide.*

☆ *Standard & Poor's Registry of Corporations, Directors, and Executives.* Listing thousands of corporations, officers, directors and trustees, this three-volume directory offers a plethora of information. Listings are indexed under a variety of headings that make it easy to search for company specialties. With a bit of sleuthing, you can also uncover background information on the "higher-ups" of a corporation, including where he/she was born or went to college.

☆ *The Thomas Register of American Manufacturers; Thomas Register Catalog File.* Look up a particular product or service, and you'll find every company that provides it in this 23-volume publication. Published annually, this reference also includes data on branch offices, capital ratings, company offices and, of course, addresses and phone numbers.

☆ *Moody's Complete Corporate Index.* If you are really interested in a lengthy description on a particular company, this publication is for you. If you want to know a company's history, Moody's provides the details— from financial information to when the company was founded.

☆ *The Million Dollar Directory.* This three-volume reference contains thousands of businesses, and the names of key personnel. Its listings are arranged alphabetically, geographically and by product classification to maximize the efficiency of your search.

☆ *Ward's Directory of Public and Private Companies.* As you might imagine, the directory lists both firms that are traded on stock exchanges and those that aren't. Each brief reference includes the company's name, address, phone number, officers, SIC code and products or services.

☆ *Annual Reports.* Publicly held corporations produce these handsome booklets to highlight their financial status, promote their products and services, and publicize their involvement in community and charitable activities. Because the firms author their own reports, they generally slant their presentation to be as positive as possible. However, they do provide a great deal of information and are worth using if you keep this intrinsic "spin" in mind.

☆ *Clipping Files.* Local and regional publications offer excellent perspectives on companies and agencies in their circulation areas. Most metropolitan newspapers have daily business sections that provide the latest news and commentary on local and global business. Many of their articles are collected for library clipping files. If you are looking for information on a local firm, you'll probably find it in one of these files.

☆ *Local Business Journals.* Many large cities also publish weekly business journals that specialize in reporting on the regional business scene. They can be especially useful for researching small to midsize companies that are privately owned and don't publish annual reports.

Once you have your company information at your fingertips, you will need a system for extracting the most valuable data in a reasonable amount of time. To write a tailored cover letter and resume, you'll need key facts and trends, not volumes of detail. The following completed sample form shows how to gather the most salient information for an organization.

If the research to target direct mail campaign companies is more work than you can abide, you might want to try the "send one resume and cover letter to everybody" approach. Just don't expect more than a 5 percent return. To increase your chances of getting a reply, do sufficient checking to be sure you have:

☆ The correct company name. Mergers and acquisitions continue to occur and names change as a result.

☆ The correct address. You would be amazed how often firms move.

☆ Your hiring manager's name and title, correctly spelled and proper gender identified. If you want to destroy an opportunity fast, misspell a name or call a man named Leslie, "Ms."

When you have determined that your names, addresses and phone numbers are correct, type them into your computer database. Then they will be easily accessible for mail-merged cover letters and follow-ups if you choose to do them.

S a m p l e   F o r m

Company/Agency Research

Name of Company   Synchronous Systems (not a real company)
Address   2200 Wendover Road, Suite 1300, Palo Alto, CA 94303
Phone Number   415-382-9900
Contact   Tom Watson
Title   Director of Client Services

1. **How old is the organization? How did it get started?**
   Company was founded in 1982 by Ben Johnson and Susan Stellerman.

2. **How has it grown: slowly, quickly, internally, by acquisition?**
   The firm has averaged an annual growth rate of 20 percent for the first five years and 8 to 10 percent since 1988. Growth has been entirely by targeting the niche market for more effective database management systems in the health care industry, especially large physician practices.

3. **What are its sales volume, annual budget, and number of employees?**
   Privately held company will not divulge this information. However, one trade journal article said the firm was in the $10 million range and employed about 100 people.

4. **What are its profit, return on investment, and market share?**
   Again, not specifically available, but the company is an acknowledged leader in its field, and I haven't found any information to indicate financial problems.

5. **Where are its plants, offices, stores, corporate headquarters?**
   Its base is in Palo Alto and it has very small sales offices in Houston, Chicago, Boca Raton, and New York.

6. **What are its products and/or services; especially major areas of concentration and new developments?**
   The company provides both database management software and record-keeping services for large physician practices and medium-size hospitals. It is currently working on increasing its usefulness to doctors by developing software and/or a service for billing insurance companies, HMOs, preferred providers programs, and medicare.

7. **Does it seem to be community spirited and/or profess an interest in cultivating its employees?**
   Based on an article I read in the *San Francisco Business Journal,* it is an avid supporter of the Ronald McDonald House and encourages its employees to

volunteer there on company time. While I didn't see any mention of specific training programs, a company that fosters voluntarism usually believes strongly in the importance of people. This is a good sign.

8. **What kinds of careers does it offer?**
Obviously, it needs computer programmers, database managers, customer service representatives and salespeople. The customer service stuff interests me the most.

9. **What specific experience, personality traits or skills do I have that might interest this company?**
My having been a physician's office administrator for several years should be of interest to them. I have managed the type of practice that represents their greatest market. I'm used to working with a variety of people in doctors' offices, including some real prima donnas. I enjoy organizing and coordinating projects, managing people, solving problems, dealing with disgruntled patients, and setting up new systems. Their expansion into medicare billing services should be a good match for my background because my office processed a lot of medicare claims for our patients.

"I must say, I'm particularly impressed with the coffee rings and eraser crumbs on your resume."

3

Resume Guidelines

N ow that you have organized your office and job-search system, developed your accomplishments history and gathered information on possible employers and job openings, you're ready to write your resume. While you can use a number of different formats or approaches (described in detail in later chapters), all resumes should adhere to the basic guidelines described in this chapter.

Tailor Your Resume to Employer Needs

Customize as much as you possibly can. This advice may seem redundant by now, but customizing your resume is the single most important thing you can do to make it successful. In fact, the reason most job hunters aren't more effective when mass-mailing resumes is that they don't address each potential employer's specific needs.

To derive the greatest benefit from your resume, consider how your past experience pertains to the position you want. Then, exclude all information that isn't relevant. Don't feel compelled to use extraneous items on the off chance that they might be remotely interesting to a prospective employer. Using a scattergun approach forces employers to hunt for experience parallel to their requirements and gives them good reasons to reject your resume altogether. If you want to land an interview, make it easy for recruiters. Provide them with what they need to know, nothing more.

ROBERT HALF'S RESUMANIA

It's fine for job seekers to include strengths on their resumes if they involve work-related skills. This Las Vegas job seeker didn't quite succeed in making a good connection. "I have an amazing memory. Once I read or hear something, I never forget it. As evidence of this, I have the ability to beat the house here in Las Vegas at 21, even if they use as many as eight decks of cards. In fact, two of the largest casinos here have prohibited me from playing."

ROBERT HALF'S RESUMANIA

A Boston man devotes most of his resume to what he has called "Strengths." Under that heading, he stresses that he is a hard-nosed, demanding manager whose eyes never left the bottom line. That isn't necessarily bad in these lean-to-mean times. But he concludes the section with the following: "I'm willing to take on the nasty tasks that others shun. For instance, I have no trouble calling employees in, looking them in the eye and telling them they're fired. In fact, I suppose you could even say I enjoy this aspect of management. It gives me gratification to know that I'm weeding out the chaff and keeping the wheat. Not only am I comfortable in this role within the company, I don't hesitate to get rid of vendors who aren't up to snuff. In the first six months of my present job, I fired the law firm, the accounting firm and the advertising agency."

By now, you may be asking, "All this tailoring is fine if I know what job I want. What if I don't know? What if a friend wants to distribute my resume to her network of contacts? Or, suppose I'm contemplating a career change and haven't decided on my new vocation? How can you expect me to customize anything under these circumstances?"

There are two answers to this question. First, if you're planning a career change, don't construct a resume until you decide what your next career will be. One of the quickest ways to guarantee your resume a spot in the reject pile is to cover a variety of unrelated bases or simply list your work history in chronological order. If you've been an accountant and you want to be a people influencer, distributing a resume that labels you as a number cruncher is deadly. Before you start your resume, conduct your research and choose your next career. Don't begin writing until you have a clear idea of your new direction. In other words, use the same process outlined in Chapter 2, but wait until you have made some important career decisions.

If you have an enthusiastic friend who wants to give your resume to lots of people, ask her if you can talk to them instead. Then you can meet with them, ascertain their needs, and tailor a resume for each contact who asks for one. If this approach is fraught with political potholes, go ahead and give her the resume she requested. But tailor it, too. Since you have no benchmark description, you'll have to create your own, and write your resume to parallel it. Granted your idealized version may not match everyone's needs, but it will mesh with yours. If you customize your resume to your own criteria, it will speak to jobs you'll enjoy and eliminate those you won't.

Rachel had been in sales for a number of years and was anxious to move into fund-raising for a large nonprofit agency. She had a friend with contacts in the nonprofit community who wanted to hand-deliver her resume to some likely employers. Because Rachel had done a lot of development work for her local Jewish Community Center, she decided to feature it on her resume instead of stressing her background in computer sales. But she was concerned about this approach. What if her resume was reviewed by someone who was anti-Semitic? He obviously wouldn't want to hire her. She would be taking herself out of the running for positions at his organization.

But, Rachel's career counselor asked—Wouldn't losing out on such opportunities be better for her? What if she weren't eliminated? Suppose this type of employer hired her, then learned of her propensity for working with "those people." How would Rachel feel about collaborating daily with a bigot? Would she want to divide her priorities between raising money for a good cause and raising his consciousness? Or would she prefer to confine her battles to just one productive front? Rachel decided to describe her experience with the Center and let the chips fall where they might. If any of her friend's contacts had a problem with her choice of volunteer assignments, both she and they would be better off not exploring the possibility of working together.

To develop your ideal job description, list the following elements:

☆ Your top 10 skills from your skills inventory.

☆ The specialized knowledge you have enjoyed developing in your paid positions, volunteer work, hobbies or classes.

☆ Your strongest personality traits.

☆ The elements you most value in your work setting such as intellectual freedom, opportunity to help others, a substantial income, teamwork, project or operations orientation, chance for advancement, variety, independence and a fast or slow pace.

☆ The salary, benefits, perks, bonuses, stock options, commissions you expect.

☆ Your intermediate and long-term career goals.

Once you have listed these criteria, synthesize them into a paragraph or two describing the activities and environment best suited to your talents, background and needs. Then, using this ideal job description as your benchmark, tailor a resume that illustrates how exquisitely qualified you are for your perfect position. Probably your ideal position won't be an exact fit with any available openings, but it should be close enough to a few opportunities to get you a courtesy interview, especially if you're recommended by a mutual friend. An example of a typical Ideal Job Description follows.

IDEAL JOB DESCRIPTION

My overriding motivation is to make a positive difference in other people's lives. I most enjoy doing this through counseling individuals, facilitating workshops and speaking on personal and professional development issues.

I'm people-oriented, goal-directed, creative and a quick thinker, so I need to move forward with cutting-edge programs that fulfill people's needs. Bureaucracy, fuzzy thinking and indecisiveness, when the well-being of people is at stake, drive me wild.

I'm best in a leadership or coaching role where I can call my own shots. I like to develop pioneering projects and use my planning, motivating, synthesizing and analytical skills to create new programs or solutions. There's nothing more fun than a successful team effort, especially when I'm the leader.

Having control over my schedule will give me the opportunity and flexibility to spend time with my family and exercise on a regular basis. A successful career is an empty triumph without good health and a happy personal life.

Use Humor Sparingly

Unless you have credentials as a stand-up comic or joke writer, be careful about including jokes in a resume. Humor is an art form best left to professionals, who, even with their experience and polish, don't always achieve the results they want.

ROBERT HALF'S RESUMANIA

"SKILLS: Possess the needed ingredients for a successful manager: One cup of ambition, a pinch of aggressiveness, two pounds of determination, one touch of integrity, one ounce of intelligence, a bit of reliability and a sprinkle of humor."

ROBERT HALF'S RESUMANIA

I'm looking at a resume right now from a gentleman whose background is solid, but who chose to use a cover sheet featuring a cartoon he drew of himself training an automatic weapon on three other cartoon characters, who are backed up against a wall, their hands raised, a look of abject terror on their faces. I think those three characters are supposed to represent wasteful spending in business, and our candidate is attempting to graphically illustrate how capable he is of holding them in check. No matter. Cartoons not only are inappropriate when seeking a job, this one happens to be offensive.

Be Brief and Concise

Have you ever received a resume that droned on for four incredibly detailed and boring pages? The person who wrote it wanted to ensure that he included everything you needed to know about his job experience. He didn't understand that resumes are similar to advertisements or brochures. Their purpose is to highlight experience and entice the potential "buyer" to get better acquainted with the product. If your resume is longer than two pages, you're not just hitting the high points—you're telling your life's story.

Picture yourself sitting at your desk, wading through a stack of resumes sent in response to a recent newspaper ad. Because this project is using valuable time that you should be spending on more immediately productive activities, you're already feeling hostile about finding a new employee. Halfway through the stack you spy a resume, heavier than most, that begins with a half-page, single-spaced dissertation on John Smith's current assignment. You're peeved that John has the audacity to assume you would be interested in the intricacies of his daily routine. With more than a little righteous indignation, you pitch his resume into the waste basket.

On the other hand, don't become overzealous in your need to be concise, or fall for the old myth that employers won't read resumes that exceed a page. For most seasoned professionals, one page isn't enough. To list your most important accomplishments may require two pages.

To keep from running long, pretend you're composing an executive brief of two pages or less describing salient points about a complicated deal. First write your rough draft, then critique it for extraneous material. Be relatively ruthless, but don't omit key elements that play an important role in substantiating your position. You want your resume to be lean, not anorexic.

Write Your Own Resume

Many resume readers scan thousands of these documents each year. They're intimately familiar with formats, typefaces and buzz words. And they can readily spot a professionally written resume. When they see one, they often question its credibility, either because it sounds too slick or they recognize its fill-in-the-blanks formula.

A resume should be a personal expression of who you are. It should represent you in a way that's both comfortable and accurate. If you think you're incapable of writing such a document, get help, but maintain control over the final product. When you're facing your interviewer, you must sound as if you wrote your resume and be conversant with everything in it. Cyrano de Bergerac won't be hiding in the bushes to coach you with optimal answers.

If the thought of writing a resume sends you into an intellectual paralysis, take heart. Chapter 4 includes a primer on how to find a professional who'll help you create a resume that highlights your best achievements, sounds as if you wrote it and prepares you to tell a potential employer in person why you're the right candidate for the job.

Be Neat and Error Free

Everyone knows that even one resume typo can destroy a candidate's credibility, yet recruiters continue to find unbelievable bloopers that serve as a continual source of black humor. These come from Robert Half:

A young lady actually sent out her resume with the following statement about herself: "I am very consiensous about my acurecy when I work."

"STRENGTHS: I am very detail oriented, and i believe in doing things wright the first time threw."

From an accountant in Seattle: "PERSONAL STRENGTHS: I am loyal, hardworking, and have plenty of patients."

The writers who produced these gaffes, while probably literate, are nonetheless careless or lack good proofreading skills. If you read what you're thinking instead of what's actually written, don't trust yourself to proofread your own resume. Give it to other people to look over as well.

Typos aren't the only glitches job seekers neglect to fix. Certain errors in grammar or sentence structure would be laughable if they didn't have serious consequences.

Prioritize Everything

Your resume should be a document that Mr. Spock would be proud to present to Starfleet Command. Its logic should be impeccable, and its ideas should flow easily from one to another in descending order of importance. What are the most critical pieces of information an employer needs to know about you? Your name, address and phone number. That's why they always appear at the top. What's the next most significant item? Your job objective, because it establishes the premise for everything else in your resume.

The order of your education, experience, personal qualifications and employment history will depend on what's most important to your potential employer. Most businesses are more concerned about your work background than your education. Consequently, it makes sense to put career accomplishments before educational credentials. However, if you're applying for a position in academia, you should emphasize your academic background, because education is an educator's bread and butter.

If you don't know who will receive your resume, prioritize according to your own preferences. Suppose you're justifiably proud of your recent MBA and certification in Total Quality Management. List these educational credentials directly under your objective. If doubling territory sales to $10 million from $5 million in the past two years is your most outstanding accomplishment, don't bury it. Put it right at the top where it grabs readers' attention.

As you plan your resume, decide first on the order of the main headings: Objective, Professional Summary, Applicable Experience, Work History, Education,

Awards and Honors, and Personal or Other Facts. Then prioritize the items under each of these major components. When finished, the information on your resume should descend logically from the most to the least important elements.

Make Your Resume Easy to Read

Sometimes well-written resumes are difficult to read because they are poorly formatted. Like a candidate during an initial interview, the impression your resume makes during the first 60 seconds will color readers' attitudes about its total content. To encourage a reader to scan your resume completely, use a format that's easy to follow.

Allowing enough white space on the page is an excellent formatting technique. Make your margins wide enough so the body of your resume won't look crowded. Leave a line of space between main headings and each of the elements below them.

Use bullets instead of long, complicated paragraphs to emphasize key points. Four lines of single-spaced text is about all a recruiter can read without getting restless. More copy can make her feel as if she's slogging through the dismal swamp. Notice the difference between the following long paragraph versus the bulleted list that presents the same information:

Team Leader, AS/400 Office Marketing   1992-present

Managed a national marketing campaign that produced sales 117% of quota. Developed advertising and PR programs using print media, trade show presentations, press interviews, brochures, video- and audiotapes, and first mail campaigns. Coordinated the efforts of team members who produced product catalogs, telemarketing programs, product documentation, and training and incentives for field salespeople and recruitment and education of distributors. "Stretched the envelope" by developing and acquiring client/server software for Mac, Windows, and OS/2 users to compliment our own offerings.

Team Leader, AS/400 Office Marketing   1992-present

- Managed a national marketing campaign that produced sales 117% of quota.
- Developed advertising and PR programs using print media, trade show presentations, press interviews, brochures, video-tapes and audiotapes, and first mail campaigns.
- Coordinated the efforts of team members who produced product catalogs, telemarketing programs, product documentation, and training and incentives for field salespeople and distributors.
- "Stretched the envelope" by developing and acquiring client/server software for Mac, Windows, and OS/2 users to compliment our own offerings.

Another way to add interest and readability is by varying typefaces, using two or three versions at most. Bold type can emphasize headings. Italic type adds punch to key words or phrases. Just be judicious when selecting typefaces. Some resumes look as if their writers have suddenly discovered a new toy. They're such a hodgepodge of type styles their message gets lost in a confusion of letters.

Probably the most important advice on format concerns the use of readable language. The KISS Principle (Keep it Simple, Stupid) is critical to a successful resume. Write as if you were talking, and leave the 50-cent words to the William Buckleys of the world who use them regularly.

ROBERT HALF'S RESUMANIA

"While I am open to the initial nature of an assignment, I am decidedly disposed that it be so oriented as to at least partially incorporate the experience enjoyed heretofore and that it be configured so as to ultimately lead to the application of the more rarefied facets of financial management as the major sphere of responsibility."

ROBERT HALF'S RESUMANIA

"OBJECTIVE: Post as data communicative expert in which coordination as an administrive responsibility in pertinence to my related background in relevance to."

"OBJECTIVE: Where the need for the ability to relate abstract concepts to clear understandable examples exists."

"EXPERIENCE: The major projects with which I have been involved include a heuristic approach to solving a three variable function to within some arbitrarily defined error using a nine point matrix, determination of the effect on next period forecasting using an exponentially weighted moving average when time periods of data are aggregated and the separate period forecasts are used to develop the next period forecast, and the method to find optimal clusters from a machine/component matrix by modifying the Direct Clustering and Bond Energy algorithms."

Omit Negative Information

While it's always advisable to be truthful on your resume, soul baring isn't mandatory. If you aren't particularly proud of something in your job history, don't mention it until the interview stage.

Imagine that you're scanning resumes in search of a new employee. How anxious would you be to meet the candidate who wrote the following Resumania item?

> PERSONAL—I am the most accurate and knowledgeable information systems expert in the company I work for. I turn out more work than any two of my colleagues put together. However, I have a time phobia that has existed since childhood. I can never get to work on time regardless of when the starting time is. But that shouldn't matter. Why should anyone care when I do my work?

Curb Your Anger

It's understandable for many job seekers to be angry and frustrated with former employers. However, it's neither fair nor wise for them to vent their feelings on future ones. This behavior falls into the "go home and kick the dog" genre of misplaced emotion.

Sometimes anger develops from anxiety and disappointment over the results of the job-search process. Having received several rejection letters, or, worse, no response at all, an unsuccessful candidate may decide to paint all potential employers with the same negative brush. Certainly, we can empathize with the disgruntled resume writer's righteous indignation. But we can't admire his negative attempt at selling himself.

No employer wants to hire a professional who hates the world. If you were looking to fill a key position in your firm, would you pick a hothead? Anger has no place in cover letters or resumes, no matter how justified it may be. Don't forget: One brief moment of self-serving vitriol can sabotage all your efforts to gain long-term satisfaction.

Don't Make Demands of the Employer

When seeking a position, it's important to know whether a potential opportunity can meet your needs. But don't mention what you want until after the recruiter has determined what you can do for him. If you make demands in your cover letter

ROBERT HALF'S RESUMANIA

"After careful consideration, I regret to inform you that I am unable to accept any refusal to offer me employment with your organization. I have been particularly fortunate this year in receiving an unusually large number of rejections. It has become impossible for me to accept any more, and your rejection would not meet with my needs at this time. Therefore employ me as soon as possible. Best of luck in employing future candidates."

"CURRENT EMPLOYMENT STATUS: At the present time I still have pending litigation against individuals, newspapers and financial firms for invasion of my privacy, harassment, criminal conspiracy, fraud, and other violations of state and federal laws that have resulted in severe damage to my personal and professional life."

"My boss is a tyrant, has no compassion at all, and has an intelligence slightly above the level of an idiot. I have a list of all our customers and suppliers, which I will bring to my new employment. I also have the home phone numbers of more than a hundred of the best employees who are anxious to join me to leave this intolerable garbage dump."

"Is this position really available or is this just some come-on to get me in your office? I don't have time for that. I also question some of the qualifications you list as being necessary. Life experience should be ranked a lot higher than education."

or resume, you're likely to be labeled as a malcontent primarily interested in what you can squeeze from the company.

Put yourself in the shoes of a potential employer who has never met the writers of the following resume excerpts. How would you feel about hiring a candidate who demands concessions before you've met him or her? If you're like most recruiters, you'll put these job seekers' resumes in the reject pile.

OBJECTIVE: Easy work, pleasant surroundings, large expense account, high wages and close to home.

OBJECTIVE: To find a job in which my education and experience will be put to optimum use, and that will appreciate the fact that I am happily married, and that my wife comes first.

To Whom It May Concern:

I am not available for many job interviews because I have very little leisure time, so any interview must be with a company that is already interested in me. In addition, the company must offer me what I am looking for. I must have in any new employment medical insurance coverage that is effective on my first day of work, and a salary to exceed what I am currently making.

I am mainly interested in working in Brooklyn, and my second choice is downtown Manhattan. If a position is offered me in Manhattan, the company will have to be a very good one and offer me no less than $10,000 more than I am currently making.

I am not a typist. I do not take shorthand. I have no experience or interest in word processing.

THE RESUME FROM HELL

Occasionally, an entire resume is bad enough to be considered for this column. This resume was written by a gentleman from Toledo, Ohio, who sought a job as a plant accountant. His resume ran on page after page, and ended with the infamous Reasons for Leaving section:

"My first job was with the XYZ Corp. I was hired to do the procedures and programming for converting their P/R to EDP. This was quite an assignment and it took two years to complete. To my amazement, when the new machine came in it was an IBM, and I had programmed the job for a Burroughs. I say this was not my fault since the memorandum from the controller advising me that they had ordered the IBM instead of the Burroughs was never received by me.

"When I left XYZ (they got awfully stuffy about the incident), I took a position with ABC Services, Inc. as a tabulating supervisor. Here I had experience in production control and inventory on EAM (had enough EDP). Their procedures were very straight forward and did not show imagination or use of the more involved aspects of machine work, so I revised them. At the end of the first year I gave them a real inventory job for a change. They never had as much information before. Naturally since it was the first year with a new system, there were some problems and the results weren't too exact. I didn't realize then how inventory and taxes are related so when the President and Chairman of the Board were both put under Federal Indictment for embezzlement, I didn't wait around. I could see the old handwriting on the wall again and started scouting around for a new position.

"I next had four or five jobs as supervisor or assistant supervisor which were not too interesting so I won't go into them.

"On my last assignment I was manager of a three-shift operation. I gained experience in time-recording and machine utilization and if they had given me time to complete my re-organization I could have whipped up a crackerjack outfit there. See, what happened was this. I was going at it one shift at a time and I shaped things up on the 1st and 2nd shift and was just starting on the 3rd. I only just then started to notice that the third shift utilization was low and this surprized me because there were always an awful lot of people leaving when I came on each morning. I was going to investigate this but unfortunately the police beat me to it. It seems that my third shift supervisor was running an open craps game and taking horse bets. It seems only two of the people [I] saw leaving were employees. Well, you know how management is always looking for a scapegoat and they picked me.

"I gained a lot of experience and I am sure you will agree I am the man for you."
NOT!

"Just out of curiosity, was there any part of my resume that you *did* like?"

4

The Parts of
Your Resume

Keeping in mind the guidelines from Chapter 3, let's take a look at how to prepare the various components of your resume, starting with the most important ones.

Your Name, Address and Phone Number

Putting your name, address and phone number at the top of your resume seems simple enough, but it may be more complicated than you think. You'll want to use an address where you can receive correspondence from employers and search firms. Should it be your home, post office box, outplacement office or an executive suite? Probably the most convenient place makes the most sense.

Should your phone number be connected to your home answering machine, place of work, outplacement office, executive suite or a temporary voice mailbox? The best option is probably the most businesslike one.

Conversing with a cacophony of barking dogs or crying children in the background tends to cramp a person's professional style. Talking in a whisper or in code so your boss won't find out you're job hunting can be awkward. And then there's the 30-second message on your answering machine that greets all callers with your imitation of Jimmy Stewart. Your friends may love your sense of humor, but will it amuse the CEO of Cyber Industries, especially when he's cut off in midsentence?

To enhance your professional image, arrange for a real person to answer your phone, saying "Mr. [or Ms.] _____'s office," if you can. Outplacement and executive suites do this automatically. If you have a private office, phone line and secretary whom you trust implicitly at work, list your work number on your resume. If these options aren't available, rent an unlimited-message voice mailbox for three months. Record a businesslike greeting and check for calls at least twice a day. You also can use your home answering machine, but give Jimmy Stewart a rest.

Your Resume Objective

Below your name, address and phone number, state a concise and specific objective. If you're applying for a position as controller of A&J Mechanical, use that job title as your objective. There are several reasons this makes sense:

☆ Using a specific job title forces you to tailor your resume. Many job seekers think a generic objective gives them a lot of latitude, rather than restricting them to a particular position. The problem with this philosophy is that an ill-defined goal leads to an ill-defined resume. To secure an interview, your resume must speak directly to the needs of each recipient. Trying to be all things to all people usually results in not being much of anything to anyone.

☆ An employer likes to see the name of his job opening and company at the top of your resume. It makes him feel special. He appreciates the extra effort it took to prepare a resume just for him. Think about the little shiver of pleasure you experience when, in conversation, someone addresses you by name, or the maître d' at your favorite restaurant says, "So good to see you this evening, Ms. Myers." Potential employers feel the same spark of recognition when you mention their name. Don't underestimate this simple, powerful tool. It rarely fails to make a positive impression.

Another effective technique when writing an objective is to include key skills that mirror important requirements mentioned in an ad or conversation with a potential employer. For instance, the accompanying ad from the *National Business Employment Weekly* says the firm is looking for a candidate who can:

☆ Develop and service new and existing accounts.

☆ Close long and short-term sales.

☆ Train and motivate others.

☆ Service a large territory under remote leadership.

If your experience includes doing any or all of these things, your objective might say:

OBJECTIVE: Account Executive for Motorola's Automotive & Industrial Electronics Group where developing and servicing new and existing accounts, closing long and short-term sales, training and motivating others and handling a large territory under remote leadership are key elements.

By using this technique, your objective becomes a summary of the most important accomplishments listed on your resume. You give the potential employer an easy and explicit bridge between what she wants in a candidate and what you offer. If you don't have bona fide background in some of the listed areas, leave them out of your objective. Otherwise you'll only serve to spotlight your deficits.

If you've had a networking appointment with a manager who has a job opening you would like to pursue, use your completed Information Interview Evaluation Form to provide ideas for enhancing your objective. In the evaluation form on page 63, the italicized phrases offer excellent clues as to what Tabor Systems wants in its employees.

After identifying the key issues of importance to Tabor, your objective might read something like this:

OBJECTIVE: Marketing Support Representative for Tabor Information Systems where a commitment to customer service, enthusiasm for adapting to changing market needs, and a desire to contribute new ideas in a team environment are prerequisites.

By recognizing the cornerstones of Tabor's corporate culture, and stating them at the top of your resume, you've grabbed the company's attention and put yourself in a position to reinforce mutual philosophy with tangible experience.

Objectives for executive search firms and direct mail campaigns are a little more difficult to formulate because you don't have a specific job title. However, if you have done your homework, you'll know the types of skills or personality traits they most appreciate. An objective for one of these potential job sources might read:

OBJECTIVE: A Financial Management position (for Baker Foods) where experience in developing new information systems for a fast-growing environment, coordinating IPO activities, troubleshooting with a number of divisions and supervising a rapidly expanding staff would be useful.

If you have no idea who will be receiving your resume, (remember the friend who has decided to become your personal agent), it's probably best to omit your

---

INFORMATION INTERVIEW EVALUATION

Person Interviewed: Susan Schmidt
Title: Manager, Marketing Support
Name of Company: Tabor Information Systems
Address: 332 Marlboro Drive
                      Fort Worth, Texas 76118
Phone Number: 817-387-2242
Secretary's Name: Melinda Daniels
Name of Person
Who Can Hire: Susan Schmidt
Date of Interview: July 3, 1994

What was my general feeling about the interview?

Susan was very accommodating. . . .

How did the interviewee respond to questions about herself?

Susan was very candid about her transition from IBM to Tabor. She said the cultures were very different, and it took her a while to adjust. She also mentioned that her *commitment to customer service* and the *many hours of training from IBM* have served her well at Tabor. She seemed very open to answering questions about her past and future, and she enjoyed musing over the state of her company and industry.

How do I feel about the company and its policies?

Tabor is a *very entrepreneurial company.* The success of the individual is predicated on her *ability and willingness to adapt to changing market demands,* while keeping *customer service at the top of her priorities.* "If these customers would leave me alone, I could finish this paperwork," is an attitude that won't fly there. I like that. *Individual ideas* are encouraged. *Teamwork and empowerment* are not just cliches. . . .

Which of my skills, personality traits, experiences mesh with what this company needs and wants?

I have the commitment to customer service and the desire to serve the client even if my quota suffers for it this quarter. I like the fact that Tabor doesn't require specific industry experience, because I consider myself to be more of a customer service generalist than a specialist. It seems *my constant ideaphoria* will serve me well here, where it has caused me problems in the past. I particularly *enjoy working with small to medium-size businesses,* which are a *major target market for Tabor.*

Can I fit into the current structure? Can I create a new job for myself? Does this company have opportunities that meet my requirements?

While the Marketing Support area is currently at full staff, Susan says her budget calls for a *new position to be added next quarter.* Given what I've seen of the company so far, I think this job would suit my skill, personality and goals. While Susan won't be leaving her job soon, she says there will be *other opportunities to move into manager slots as the company expands across the United States and into Mexico. I speak Spanish* and the *chance to live in a foreign country is very appealing.*

What should I do to follow up on this information interview?

Of course, I'll send a thank-you note and resume. . . .

objective altogether. While this approach certainly isn't ideal, it's better than using such a conglomeration of pablumlike phrases as:

OBJECTIVE: Seeking an opportunity for advancement in a dynamic, growth-oriented company where my hands-on management style will produce bottom-line results.

Robert Half's quotations illustrate the principle that a poorly conceived objective is far worse than none at all.

ROBERT HALF'S RESUMANIA

"OBJECTIVE: To work with real people again."

"OBJECTIVE: To have something to do."

"OBJECTIVE: To work for a strong, prosperous company in a professional environment as an internal auditor with opportunities for advancement and the potential of creating a union on inculcated academic ideals with practical and tangible objectivity."

"OBJECTIVE: Cash for talent."

"OBJECTIVE: A management position in which I can make order out of chaos and evil."

"GOAL: Get out of a rut."

"OBJECTIVE: To inject Faith, Hope and Charity into the American workplace."

"OBJECTIVE: A position in which I can run the whole shootin' match."

"OBJECTIVE: I am anxious to work for your company."

"OBJECTIVE: To make money and have fun."

"GOAL: It's my ambition and challenge, just to summarize my position, to simultaneously confirm and formulate a consistently profitable, coherent and emotionally rewarding career."

The Professional Qualifications Brief (Summary of Qualifications)

This part of your resume summarizes the most important skills, experience and personality traits you have to offer a prospective employer. For maximum impact, you must tailor it to the specific job you seek and provide a unique commentary on who you are and what you can do. This four-to-six phrase section should capture your professional essence. It is your 30-second commercial. Lavish on it all the attention and care General Motors Corporation would put into a Super Bowl ad.

Go back to the drawing board, though, if your first attempt at a summary sounds like this:

PERSONAL QUALIFICATIONS: A demonstrated record of achievement, leadership and hard work.

A dedicated, highly motivated team member.

Work well under pressure.

A people person.

If you can't say something special about yourself, omit this section and move directly to "Experience."

The two Qualifications Briefs that follow work well with their job objectives because their authors have carefully customized them to a specific position or career. While the briefs are quite different, they speak volumes about their writers in just a few short phrases.

OBJECTIVE

A senior-level position where experience in product development and sales in international markets would be valuable.

PERSONAL QUALIFICATIONS

• Eighteen years of front-line management experience in marketing and selling international products and services.

• Extensive understanding of global socioeconomics.

• A transcultural individual who is comfortable with people and settings around the world.

• Skilled at bringing a diversity of people together to pursue a common goal whether within my firm or among partner institutions.

• Willing to relocate abroad.

OBJECTIVE

Director of Development for the Save Our Forest Foundation.

PERSONAL QUALIFICATIONS
- Many contacts in the academic, social service and corporate communities, cultivated over the past 15 years.
- Expert in designing and presenting proposals and training programs.
- Easily establish rapport with people of all ages, cultures, and philosophies.
- Skilled in organizing events.
- Active member of the Sierra Fund for the past 10 years.

ROBERT HALF'S RESUMANIA

"PERSONALITY PROFILE: Gemini-Mercurial personality, extremely witty, charming, kind, loving, sociable and with a light, easy-going disposition. I'm a super salesman, as well as a wonderful executive who creates systems that work. I am determined to succeed. I work hard. I have sound judgment and a ton of common sense and drive. I believe in action, and positive thinking. I do business best with Aquarius and Aries personalities."

"AREAS OF COMPETENCE: Demonstrated responsibilities to plan, direct, develop, evaluate and expedite all operations. I possess the ability to make sound judgments, influence people, organize, persuade and motivate them to produce and achieve their goals. I am ambitious, self-motivated and industrious. Besides being trustworthy, honest and diplomatic, I communicate well with others, and plan and present ideas. Some of my older attributes are assertiveness, consistency and tenacity. Dominance, achievement, autonomy, intraception and heterosexuality are my many traits."

"My most attractive qualification is the ability to get to the heart of a problem. I have a mind that most people say is highly analytical. One person I worked with even called my mind a steel trap. When you combine my personal appearance and communication skills with my ability to analyze a problem and solve it in record time, you'll agree that I am a very attractive find for any employer looking for the cream of the crop."

"QUALIFICATIONS: No, I am not the typical job seeker you deal with on a regular basis whose resume fits perfectly into the expanding global strategy of a well-oiled, competitive multinational corporate leader."

Experience

There are many ways to put together an experience section. However, the following tips are essential.

Talk About Your Accomplishments Rather Than Your Responsibilities

If a company employs three people with the same job description, one may be exceptional, another may be only mediocre and the third may be downright incompetent. If all three listed only duties or responsibilities on their resumes, a recruiter wouldn't be able to detect any difference among them.

You can spotlight your capabilities by selecting and expanding on specific achievements that reflect your initiative, creativity, follow-through, problem-solving and management skills. The following are before-and-after versions of an IBM employee's credentials as Senior Marketing Support Representative:

Before

- Conducted national marketing campaigns.
- Introduced new products into the marketplace.
- Defined market requirements for development.
- Trained and supported the field and companies selling our products.
- Developed additional distribution channels.
- Recruited additional companies to develop complementary offerings.
- Advised customers on which platform (host, midrange or PC) to develop applications.
- Managed development of software tool used to analyze computer performance.

After

- Advised customers and IBM salespeople concerning the best hardware and software solutions for their requirements.
- Member of the team that introduced the AS/400, IBM's biggest worldwide rollout in 1988. Led the effort to compare the AS/400 with other computer systems and presented the results at IBM's national kickoff.
- Managed development of a software tool used by salespeople to analyze the performance requirements of user systems. This tool has been applied to thousands of systems nationwide and generated an IBM "Excellence" award.
- Served as an advisor and coordinator for the Director in charge of the worldwide announcement of OfficeVision software, IBM's biggest worldwide product launch in 1989.
- Worked on a task force with high-level executives to determine future plans for IBM in the software marketplace.

Which do you find more impressive: the basic job description or the summary of key accomplishments?

Always Use Action Verbs to Begin Each Achievement

Action verbs add sizzle and punch to your resume. When you review your completed skills inventory from Chapter 2, you'll note that it's full of these verbs. Use them when formulating your Experience section. The accompanying list of examples should help you get started:

Administered	Designed	Negotiated
Advised	Developed	Organized
Analyzed	Directed	Persuaded
Appraised	Edited	Planned
Arranged	Established	Presented
Budgeted	Estimated	Recruited
Chaired	Evaluated	Represented
Coached	Explained	Researched
Collaborated	Facilitated	Reviewed
Contacted	Improved	Sold
Cooperated	Instructed	Supervised
Coordinated	Investigated	Updated
Counseled	Lead	Visualized
Created	Learned	Wrote
Decided	Managed	

Remember: Too much of a good thing is too much, as shown by a Santa Fe, New Mexico resume writer who took the action verb idea to the extreme. The first page of his resume listed these items: *Catapulted* sales of new product . . . *Captured* multimillion dollar contract . . . *Slashed* expenses . . . *Sparked* large increase in revenue . . . *Propelled* profitability . . . *Spearheaded* projects . . . and *Pioneered* the development of . . .

This description sounds more like Attila the Hun's battle plan than the activities of a typical account executive.

Do Not Use the Pronoun "I"

Refrain from using the pronoun "I" or referring to yourself as "the candidate" when listing your achievements. The reader knows whose resume she's reading.

Quantify Your Accomplishments Whenever Possible

There's something about numbers that catches people's attention and helps them to understand the scope of your work. Items to be quantified include sales revenue, inventory turns, worker hours or dollars saved, clients or other employees served, states covered by your region, percentage reduction in plant accidents or claims filed, widgets produced, funds raised and so on. Here are some examples:

- Managed a program that trained 120 adults per year for competitive employment.
- Supervised a staff of 60.
- Developed proposals for funding that resulted in 100% increase in program funds.
- Sold and serviced approximately 100 wholesalers, manufacturers, major retail chains and independent stores throughout the Southwest.
- Administered an annual budget of $1.2 million.

If your achievements don't easily translate into numbers, try mentioning names instead. Listing projects where you worked with the CEO, an important political figure, a VP or a well-known sports personality may score you some points. If your company's or clients' names are particularly impressive, use them unless it would be unethical or inappropriate to do so. For instance, you might say:

- Worked in collaboration with all of Nabisco's regional managers to formulate a new long-range management incentive plan.
- Managed all public relations activities for the Byron Nelson Golf Classic.
- Provided customer service for Midwestern key accounts including Xerox, GM, the Post Office, WR Grace, and Exxon, among others.

Use Appropriate Jargon

Using the correct jargon for the industry and company you are courting is especially important for career changers who might be unclear about the meaning of relatively esoteric words.

A good illustration of how the wrong jargon can sabotage you: What is the term that describes speaking to impart knowledge in front of a classroom full of attendees? In elementary schools and high schools, the activity is known as teaching. In a social service setting, it's called facilitating. At a college or university, it's instructing. And in a business environment, it's training. Don't ever confuse a teacher with a trainer (the teacher may tell you that trainers work with animals, not children). And, when businesspeople hear the word facilitator, they think of a bleeding-heart social worker, not a savvy, profit-oriented professional.

Don't Separate Volunteer or Other Unpaid Experience from Paid Achievements, If It's Relevant to the Job You're Seeking

In your accomplishments history, you included all the experience you deemed satisfying and worthwhile. Regardless of whether your experience is paid, volunteer, hobby, professional organization or daily life activity, it deserves a place on your resume if it relates to your job objective.

Unfortunately, money and value seem to be synonymous in our culture. This attitude is wrong, but must be dealt with nonetheless. Getting credit for your unpaid work may require using a functional rather than a chronological format. Here's how a teacher included volunteer accomplishments as well as paid ones among her relevant experiences:

PROJECT MANAGEMENT

• Chaired seven receptions honoring retirees and volunteers. Approximately 200 people attended each event.

• Served as Chairman of the Public Relations committee that organized and implemented a charity softball game for the Kent Waldrep National Paralysis Association. Players included members of the Dallas Cowboys and the Dallas media.

• Organized a field day for 300 people that required working with staff and volunteers, finding in-kind services, planning games, logistics and an awards ceremony.

• Facilitated or found speakers for over 50 training programs for administration, staff and parents of the Richardson Independent School District.

• Developed a variety of volunteer programs for parents who helped with field trips, field days, classroom activities and parties.

• Created and taught a pilot kindergarten program for RISD. Designed the physical environment, planned curriculum, started a parent volunteer program, budgeted and ordered supplies.

Hobbies are valid achievements, too, especially if they enhance your job objective. Suppose you're an art teacher who has been belly dancing for years to stay in shape. After careful thought, you decide to make belly dancing a career (yes, this is a true example). You realize that having a resume that describes your educational credentials won't inspire confidence in your ability to amuse a crowd of partying adults. Instead of concentrating on your paid career, you list a variety of venues where you danced in front of groups. Toward the bottom of your Experience section, you allude to your ability to hold a group's attention and foster its enthusiastic participation based on your years of working with teenagers. However, you don't list this skill first.

Use Dates If They're in Your Favor

Some job seekers have "perfect" employment records that show progressively increasing responsibilities. They have never been laid off or worked at home to raise children, and have stayed at each job for three or more years. For these candidates, listing employment dates in reverse chronological order works nicely. However, a growing number of people have gaps in their employment history, have held numerous jobs or need to list their previous positions in order of importance instead of with their most recent jobs first. If you're one of them, consider stating the number of years you held the job instead of employment dates, or omitting employment dates and length of employment altogether.

Unfortunately, some employers discount candidates whose resumes show that they've stayed at one company for an extended period, or whose work histories portray them as seasoned veterans (in the workforce 20 years or more, 40 years old or older). If you're in either of these categories, providing specific dates may not be to your advantage.

There are several ways to categorize experience without focusing on dates. Older professionals may decide to omit the first few jobs on their resumes, thereby reducing their employment histories. This technique isn't likely to force them to omit their most important accomplishments. Now will it reveal their ages.

Older candidates also can list their experience by job title, giving the number of years worked for each position instead of the dates of employment. If you choose this method, put your employment time span in a relatively inconspicuous place. For instance, you might try this approach:

Purchasing Manager   Crawford Technologies   Omaha, NE   Five years

Using a functional format also allows you to catalog your most important accomplishments without marrying them to specific job titles and dates. The following functional experience module pulls together related activities:

PROJECT MANAGEMENT AND ADMINISTRATION
  • Developed and implemented companywide employee survey for corporate office and three manufacturing plants.
  • Researched the market and selected a consultant to do communications workshops based on the above survey results.
  • Coordinated innovative programs to encourage productivity, including:
      —Monthly bonuses to plant with the best safety record.
      —Quarterly bonuses to plant with highest productivity of board feet of foam insulation.
      —Plant employee of the year.

Education

Education may be listed before experience if:

  ☆ Your objective requires a specific credential.
  ☆ Your educational background is stronger than your work history.

First-time job seekers often have freshly minted degrees, but not much applicable experience, to offer potential employers. They should focus on their education by listing it near the top of their resumes.

Professionals applying for careers in academia also need to give priority to their educational credentials because credentialing is the main purpose of their industry. They should also include references to ongoing coursework in their field of expertise. If they're seeking instructor or professor positions, they'll want to mention research papers, speeches to professional groups and other accomplishments generally not included on a typical resume.

Most other workers can assume that experience is more important to potential employers than education. Consequently, education usually follows experience in most resumes.

Your education section may include formal degrees, noncredit courses at colleges or universities, in-house training programs, or informal learning experiences such as travel, tutoring or extensive reading in a subject. The following example of a typical education section mentions all these qualifications:

EDUCATION

MBA, Northwestern University, 1982

BSBA, The Pennsylvania State University, 1975

Continuing education courses in Total Quality Management, Covey's Leadership Training, Negotiating for Win-Win Results

Extensive reading on global socioeconomic issues

If you're planning to change careers and your major has little to do with your new objective, list only the degree level and omit your field of study. If your degree is more than 10 years old, leave out the graduation date. In many instances, your level of education tells more about your ability to persevere than your expertise in a given subject. If your degree has become obsolete or doesn't relate to your career, there's no need to emphasize it.

Organizations

Potential employers look favorably on candidates who are active participants in organizations. Your involvement in such activities as PTA, church, social service agency board of directors, professional association, alumni club, ecological society or city commission shows your willingness to participate in a worthy cause or help your profession. It also demonstrates that volunteer groups trust you to follow through on your commitments. Businesses need professionals who want to pursue a common mission, are capable and interested in assuming leadership roles, and know how to gain the respect and cooperation of their peers. Your organizational activities speak to your skills in all these areas.

Companies also realize they can bask in your reflected glory when you're chosen for a responsible position in a community or professional group. Your high profile and superb leadership only serve to reinforce what a good decision they made in hiring you. These associations also can provide you and your company with the valuable contacts needed to develop business opportunities and gain greater visibility within your industry, profession and community.

If you've played an active role in any worthwhile organization, don't hesitate to include it on your resume or use your fellow participants as references. Employers regard your ongoing commitment and contribution to these groups as both a confirmation of your competence and a proving ground for your talent.

Awards

Writing a resume gives you a mandate for talking about how wonderful you are. If other people have already honored you by selecting you for a Who's Who directory, Woman of the Year, the President's Award or other kudo, tell your potential employer about it. This is no time to be modest.

If your award is for an accomplishment within the context of your job, put it in your experience section instead of toward the end of your resume. Sales Associate of the Year is too important a distinction not to be read early on.

Personal Data

Experts offer conflicting advice about whether to include personal information on a resume. Many say to omit it altogether. Some think that listing hobbies and volunteer work gives employers a better picture of a candidate. Others suggest mentioning personal information only if it improves your chances of landing an interview. All typically agree that references to age, marital status, number of children, health, physical characteristics, as well as other types of demographic data, rarely belong on a resume unless they are a bona fide occupational qualification (BFOQ).

If you decide to include personal facts, always put them at the bottom of your resume. Even if your share a love of sailing with the recruiter, it can't be as relevant to the job as your experience or education, unless you'll be running a marina.

ROBERT HALF'S RESUMANIA

"PERSONAL: I had two children by my first wife, both live with me, but she also had two children by her second husband. One lives with his former wife, and one with my first wife. My second, and present wife, had one child by each of her first two husbands, and we had two kids together. All of those are living with us. That presently makes a total of six, but my wife is now pregnant with twins."

"PERSONAL: Married for 26 years, quit smoking 11 years ago, never had a drink, have been a gambler all my life."

"PERSONAL: 34 years old, one daughter, 9, currently entering bankruptcy proceedings."

"WHO AM I? I am 43, married for the third time and have a two-day-old son who remains nameless."

"HEALTH: I am healthier than most men half my age. I do, however, wear two hearing aids. To some, this may be considered a disadvantage. On the contrary, because I am a workaholic, I simply remove both aids when I am in the middle of a difficult project."

"Interests include: universalism, pacifism, humanism, longevity, open-minded, liberal-thinking people, lectures, meditation and any other personal growth experience. I'm allergic to smoke and wiseguys."

Salary History

Including your salary history on your resume isn't a good idea. If it's too high or too low, you'll automatically be eliminated from consideration. Even if it's in the ballpark, a salary amount mentioned early in the get-acquainted process can inhibit your ability to negotiate for what you want later on. Salary is one of those subjects best discussed face-to-face once you and your potential employer are almost ready to close the deal.

If an ad requests that you send a salary history with your resume, but you believe that including one will jeopardize your candidacy, don't send it. You may

ROBERT HALF'S RESUMANIA

The individual who sent this resume hails from Milwaukee and was looking for an internal auditor job. His background included having worked for a wine company in California, and a brewery in Milwaukee. Under SALARY HISTORY he listed the following: "Abe Wine Company—$30,000 plus 20 cases of wine. XYZ Brewery—$33,000 plus 25 cases of beer."

Fair enough, but then he went on to list areas of the country to which he'd consider moving, "First choice—Milwaukee or Minneapolis/St. Paul area. Relocation to other areas considered on a *case-by-case* basis."

"SALARY NEEDED: I have one kid in college now, another one to enter next year, and two more coming up a few years after that. This translates to $46,000 this year, $70,000 next year and who knows after that. In other words, I can't work for peanuts."

"SALARY DESIRED: $80,000, which is what my wife currently earns."

be rejected anyway for not following instructions, but you won't be any worse off. If an employer is genuinely interested in you, excluding salary information usually won't stop you from getting an interview.

Reason for Leaving

As noted in an earlier chapter, being laid off or fired because of a hostile takeover, downsizing, acquisition or difference in management philosophy will or has already occurred to most people at one time or another. You needn't be embarrassed or defensive about it.

But no matter how you explain it in a resume, you may put yourself in a no-win situation because potential employers tend to identify with former ones. Unless an ad specifically asks you for this information, don't offer it. Delay the subject until you have built some personal rapport with your interviewer. Then he will be more likely to combine this part of your conversation with his overall perspective, instead of making it the focus of a preconceived opinion.

ROBERT HALF'S RESUMANIA

"When they recruited me, it was red carpet all the way. Then they pulled the rug out on me."

"Gunned down in a political crossfire."

From a person who had left a position with a City Opportunity Council: "No Opportunity."

"Didn't know what I was doing."

"To escape this terrible town, where a beer bust is considered a big evening. Nobody plays bridge and I am bored stiff. I do not want to work for any division of this company because their accounting practices are different from concepts that let me sleep at night. Help! Get me out of here."

"Embezzlement." (He worked for a bank, and was on probation.)

"My complete mastery of the software interface was undermined by jealous peers. You can see the whole story when I sell the screenplay."

"REASON FOR LEAVING: It had to do with the IRS, FBI and SEC."

"So my ex-wife couldn't attach my wages in our divorce settlement."

"The company made me a scapegoat, just like my three previous employers did. This company would be out of business if it weren't for me. Nobody here seems to know what is going on, and I am the only one who does. Despite that, they treat me like an alien, and I am fed up with it. I think I'd better get out of here before they ask me to turn water into wine."

"NOTE: Please do not misconstrue my 14 jobs as 'job-hopping.' I have never quit a job."

References

Don't include references on your resume unless they're famous and admired. People's names, addresses and phone numbers take up a lot of space and usually have little meaning to a potential employer.

Only when you become a finalist for an opening should you give your list of references to an employer. But before you do, call your references to explain the position for which you're being considered and what the interviewer will probably want to know about you. By using this technique, you will be tailoring your references' responses to the job you're seeking and giving them some valuable time to think about what they want to say.

When choosing references, include people who know you from other walks of life besides work. In our litigious society, many employers instruct managers not to discuss your record even if it's exemplary. This means that if you only use former managers or colleagues as references, they may not be able to say anything about you, good or bad.

Other excellent references include colleagues you've worked or volunteered with, friends, bankers, ministers, golf partners, or anyone who knows you well and can articulate why you would be a welcome addition to an organization. Under no circumstances should you list people who might disparage your reputation.

ROBERT HALF'S RESUMANIA

REFERENCES: Don't take their comments too seriously. They were unappreciative beggars and slave drivers.

How to Find Resume Help

If thinking about tackling your resume and cover letters all by yourself gives you a severe case of writer's block, don't despair: Professional help is available—lots of it, representing a continuum from truly awful to sublimely perfectionistic. To find a good service and protect yourself from incompetent and unethical ones, rely on the same techniques that characterize a successful job search:

☆ Ask your friends, fellow job seekers, volunteer colleagues, church members and so forth if they can recommend a good resume service. Review a resume produced by their resource and ask how effective it was.

☆ Call the continuing education departments and community counseling services at local colleges to inquire about resume-writing courses or person-to-person counseling for nonstudents. If they provide these services, make sure they use a tailored, businesslike approach. You don't want a warmed-over, fill-in-the-blank version of a student resume, or a 5- to 10-page academic vitae.

☆ Check out nonprofit agencies such as the YMCA, YWCA, church-sponsored job club, state employment commission or private industry council job-training program to see if resume help is provided. At many nonprofits, volunteer professionals provide assistance for free or on a sliding scale based on your ability to pay.

☆ Call resume services and career counselors listed in the phone book, and ask them the following questions:

—How does your service work? Do you tailor resumes to individual positions or careers, or do you write one resume and make mulitiple copies?

—How do you obtain client information and prepare resumes? Does the client work with you? Do you use an accomplishments form and extrapolate from it? Do you have a fill-in-the-blanks computer program?

—How do your resumes look? Do you have a specific format? Do you customize fonts? Can you send me a couple of examples? Do you use a laser printer?

—What other services do you offer? Do you prepare envelopes and cover letters? Can you mail the resumes for me? Can you do a mail merge if I need one?

—What is your turnaround time? Will you give me the computer disk containing my resume if I request it? What is your price schedule?

—How would you approach writing a resume for clients who don't have specific career goals?

Many services can give you the resume support you want, but be finicky. Shop around until you find a resource that produces tailored, professional-looking resumes at moderate prices in a reasonable time frame, only makes promises it can keep and treats you like a valued client. You deserve nothing less.

"Just drop your resume into the slot and we'll be in touch."

5

The Chronological Format

The chronological resume is the type most people use. It's the traditional format that lists last position first, then rolls back in time until the final job mentioned is the first one out of school. The assumption, and rationale, behind this approach is that you'll be given increasingly responsible positions as you move through your career. Consequently, your most recent job should be your highest level one.

The main difference between the chronological format and other types of resumes is the Experience section. Chronological resumes always use job titles, company names, locations and dates as the framework for discussing your career. As with any format, this method has it pros and cons.

The Good News

Chronological resumes are readily accepted by everyone. This traditional, conservative format is comfortable for all employers. In fact, some professionals in executive search, human resources and technical fields discount any other type of resume when they seek candidates. They want to see dates because they assume that job hunters who don't include them are trying to hide something. From their point of view, good, solid candidates don't need to disguise their employment history.

A chronological resume makes an excellent showcase for someone with a perfect career, who has been promoted with every move, whose work history has no gaps and who has changed firms enough to develop a broad perspective, but not enough to be classified as a job-hopper. In this format, the last position—placed at the top of the resume—is the premier experience. The dates march smartly down the page and are sequential from one assignment to the next. And there's evidence of sufficient movement among employers to show ongoing marketability and adaptability to different corporate cultures.

The chronological format is easy to follow because it's structured on a job-by-job basis. You don't have to do much synthesizing to put it together.

The Bad News

Unfortunately, not everyone looking for a job has a perfect work history. The following types of candidates will have significant problems with this format because of their backgrounds:

☆   Parents who have taken time off to raise children.

☆   Individuals whose job searches have dragged on for months or even years.

☆   Workers who have spent time recovering from an accident or illness or caring for a sick child, spouse or parent.

☆   Those who take a year off to see the world before increasing responsibility prohibits it.

☆   Professionals who have had to make frequent job changes because their employers went bankrupt, closed offices or departments to cut overhead, or were devoured in mergers or hostile takeovers.

☆   People who transfer to lower-level jobs to stay with their companies.

☆   Job seekers who are forced to take lower-level positions to survive, because they couldn't find better opportunities before their savings or unemployment expired.

☆ Career changers who have chosen to leave long-held professions to start over in different fields.

☆ Seasoned professionals who have worked continuously for one corporation but were terminated to improve the bottom line.

The chronological format may do these job seekers more harm than good because it spotlights career steps they would like to ignore. A functional or hybrid approach will probably work better for them unless they decide to rely primarily on ads, search firms, personnel departments and conservative thinkers to help them secure new positions. If candidates with nontraditional career paths use only traditional methods of finding employment, they will, out of necessity, back themselves into a chronological corner, whether the format suits them or not.

Before-and-After Examples

This section includes some examples of good resumes that, with a little revision, became outstanding ones. Take a look at the "before" and "after" versions of each one and think about how you might apply the same suggestions to your resume.

Bill Smith

While Bill's resume begins with a concise objective, his experience section needs work. His first two positions aren't explained. This omission leads readers to believe that Bill must have been coasting for the past few years. His other jobs list his duties and responsibilities, not his accomplishments. There's probably some juicy stuff lurking behind those bland phrases, but you're hard-pressed to figure out what it is.

As a 15-year veteran of IBM, Bill has had access to an array of ongoing training programs, yet his education section only mentions a degree from the University of Texas at Dallas. Either he hasn't taken advantage of IBM's courses or doesn't give himself credit for taking them on his resume. In a field where technology renders three-year-old information worthless, continuing education is vital to a successful career.

Bill Smith
2833 Meandering Way
Houston, TX 77058
713/281-4939
713/372-6246

OBJECTIVE

Executive Information Systems Position for a company implementing applications on PC and/or midrange systems.

PROFESSIONAL EXPERIENCE

IBM Corporation 1978–1993

Team Leader, AS/400 Office Marketing (Roanoke, TX) 1992–Present

Consulting Marketing Support Representative (Roanoke, TX) 1990–1991

Senior Marketing Support Representative (Las Colinas, TX) 1988–1989
— Conducted national marketing campaigns.
— Introduced new products into the marketplace.
— Defined market requirements for development.
— Trained and supported the field and companies selling our products.
— Developed additional distribution channels.
— Recruited additional companies to develop complementary offerings.
— Advised customers on which platform (host, midrange, or PC) to develop applications.
— Managed development of software tool used to analyze computer performance.

Senior Financial Analyst (White Plains, NY) 1986–1987
— Coordinated special deals for customers who bought large quantities of products.
— Formulated creative alternatives and negotiated solutions.
— Presented and won approval from corporate directors.
— Analyzed customer requirements for future products.
— Taught Profit and Loss analysis at IBM's school for people who price IBM's products.

Advisory Planner (Atlanta, GA) 1984–1985
— Planned and negotiated product volumes, revenue, and head count for my division.
— Conducted a study that evaluated the profitability of the products sold by our division.
— Conducted a study that evaluated the affordability of IBM's long-term plans for operations in the United States.
— Evaluated and recommended to executives—marketing, productivity, and customer support programs.

Midrange Systems Specialist (Mobile, AL) 1978–1983
— Sold, installed, converted, provided technical support and training for customers on IBM computer systems.

EDUCATION
— 1977, received Bachelor of Science Degree in Business and Public Administration from the University of Texas at Dallas, graduated cum laude.

PERSONAL
— Committee leader which successfully got my community to approve a sales tax increase for building recreational facilities.
— Served on board of directors for organization that conducts youth sports programs in my community.
— Created and organized sports camps for youth in my community.
— Coached youth and adult teams in several sports.

In his improved resume, Bill has added a summary of qualifications that highlights his most relevant experience, skills and personality traits. His objective, summary and first two job descriptions cover most of the first page. They deserve this prime location because they are his "biggest guns."

Instead of listing job responsibilities, Bill has added both substance and sizzle to his experience by citing his most important accomplishments. "Managed a national marketing campaign that produced sales 117% of quota" certainly makes a bigger impact than "Conducted national marketing campaigns."

Note that Bill has also beefed up his education section by including the IBM courses he thinks employers would want him to have.

While this resume takes two pages instead of one, it more than doubles Bill's value to a company seeking a sales and marketing professional. This is a good example of how using a one-page resume, when you really need two pages, is penny-wise and pound foolish.

After

Bill Smith
2833 Meandering Way
Houston, TX 77058
713-281-4939
713-372-6246

OBJECTIVE

Executive Information Systems Position for a company implementing applications on PC and/or midrange systems.

SUMMARY

Demonstrated vision, leadership and organizational skills through:
— Coordinating Successful, Innovative National Marketing Campaigns
— Designing and Creating Information Systems
— Analyzing Profitability and Productivity of Key Departments
— Increasing the Role and Importance of Customer and Field Support Operations

PROFESSIONAL EXPERIENCE

Spent 15 years with IBM in increasingly responsible positions at headquarters and in the field. Gained diverse experience in marketing, sales, technical support and financial planning.

Team Leader, Office Products   **1992–Present**
— Managed a national marketing campaign that produced sales 117% of quota.
— Developed advertising and PR programs using print media, trade show presentations, press interviews, brochure, videotapes and audiotapes, and direct mail campaigns.
— Coordinated the efforts of team members who produced product catalogs, telemarketing programs, product documentation, training and incentives for field salespeople, and recruitment and education of distributors.
— "Stretched the envelope" by developing and acquiring client/server software for Mac, Windows, and OS/2 users to complement our own offerings.

Consulting Marketing Support Representative   **1990–1991**
— Ran a direct mail and teleselling campaign that increased sales over 6%, resulting in an IBM Vice President's award.
— Created and implemented an innovative marketing program that significantly increased product visibility and national sales by 15%.
— Received another IBM Vice President's award for this effort.
— Transformed our department group from a sales support function to a proactive marketing organization.

Senior Marketing Support Representative   **1988–1989**
— Served as an adviser and coordinator for the Director in charge of the worldwide announcement of OV Software, IBM's biggest worldwide product launch in 1989.
— Member of the team that introduced the AS/400, IBM's biggest worldwide product rollout in 1988. Led the effort to compare the AS/400 with other computer systems and presented the results at IBM's national kickoff.

Bill Smith   Page 2

— Managed development of a software tool used by salespeople to analyze the performance requirements of proposed user systems. This tool has been used for thousands of systems nationwide and generated an IBM "Excellence" award.
— Worked on a task force with high-level executives to determine future plans for IBM's role in the software marketplace.
— Advised customer and IBM salespeople concerning the best hardware and software solutions for their requirements.

Senior Financial Analyst   **1986–1987**
— Managed all customer proposals for our newest product.
— Formulated creative alternatives and negotiated solutions for new multimillion-dollar contracts.
— Won approval from corporate directors for these proposals.
— Analyzed customer requirements for future products.
— Determined product specifications and hardware and software prices.
— Taught Profit and Loss analysis at IBM's school for people who price IBM's products.

Advisory Planner   **1984–1985**
— Planned and negotiated product volumes, revenue, and head count for my division.
— Analyzed and recommended the viability of national marketing, customer support, and productivity programs.
— Conducted a study that evaluated the profitability for the products sold by our division. Met with the president and division executives to review and make recommendations for the future, based on this study.
— Evaluated the affordability of IBM's longer term plans for operations in the United States.

Midrange Systems Specialist   **1978–1983**
— Sold, installed and converted computer systems. Provided technical support and training for customers.
— Elected president of my training class at IBM.
— Selected to attend IBM's National Achievement Conference first two years eligible.
— Received numerous awards for marketing successes.

EDUCATION
— Completed continuing education courses on Managing the Media, Public Speaking and Presenting Effectively, Professional Writing, Creativity, Quality, Empowerment, Teamwork, People Management, Leadership, Profit and Loss Management and Project Management.
— Postgraduate work on MBA at the University of Dallas.
— 1977, Bachelor of Science, Business & Public Administration, University of Texas at Dallas, graduated cum laude (Note: Graduated with honors even though I worked and went to school full time.)

PERSONAL ACCOMPLISHMENTS
— Spearheaded a successful tax-increase initiative for building recreational facilities in my community.
— Served on board of directors for the Kestler Youth Group, which conducts youth sports programs.
— Created and organized the first soccer and basketball camps for youth in my community.
— Coached youth and adult teams in several sports.

David P. Kaiser

David Kaiser's "before" resume is a good one, but it is too long and wordy. To capture and hold the attention of most readers, especially those who are screening hundreds of candidates, David needs to cut his three pages down to two. What would you delete if you were he?

Revamping David's resume was easy because his overall approach was sound. By deleting half of his summary and all of his "achieved these results through managing . . ." sections, he cut 50 percent of the verbiage without any negative affect. (By the way, David recently started a new position as VP of Commercial Underwriting for USF&G, a step up from his previous job.)

Before

David P. Kaiser

Summary
Senior-level manager of commercial property-liability insurance underwriting operations. Nineteen years of experience with a top-twenty U.S. insurer. A proven leader who has successfully created and managed innovative programs and coverages for target markets and who has achieved outstanding profit and premium growth. A results-oriented individual with extensive experience in managing corporate and regional office underwriting operations whose track record in expense management, customer service and delivery of high quality insurance products and services is exceptional.

Experience includes developing and managing new programs and products, achieving a return on equity in excess of 15% and annual written premium of $3 million to $60 million for each of these target markets:

- computer services and software
- educational institutions
- financial services
- high technology manufacturers
- hospitality, recreation and leisure

- limousine operators
- medical equipment manufacturers
- museums
- oil field services
- social services

Employment History

1973–1992: St. Paul Fire and Marine Insurance Company
A property and liability insurance company with annual premium of $3 billion, a member of The St. Paul Companies, a worldwide insurance organization.

May 1988 to March 1992: Senior Underwriting Officer
Commercial Insurance Division, Corporate Headquarters
Head of the Business Development Department, one of four departments within the division; managing a staff of twelve and a budget of $1.3 million. This division is responsible for $750 million in written premium, approximately 25% of the company's total.

Results
- Increased annual premium in target markets from $48 million to $175 million by creating and managing new target market programs and coverages.
- Produced an estimated ultimate loss ratio under 50% with a resulting return on equity of over 15%.

Achieved these results through managing . . .
- research and development, including study of target markets, buyer, agent/ broker needs analyses; creating coverage forms, underwriting guidelines, marketing strategies; tailored risk management and claim services to identified target market specifications; statistical record keeping and policy issuing systems requirements
- implementation, initial underwriting and marketing of targeted market programs
- training seminars for underwriting departments, agents, brokers and insurance buyers
- $10 million in national group insurance program for banks

July 1986 to May 1988: Commercial Insurance Underwriting Manager
New England Service Center, Springfield, MA

Managed the commercial insurance underwriting department: a staff of thirty-six in two offices; $60 million in premium; a six-state territory.

Results

- Turned around an operation that was unprofitable with declining premium volume.
- Reduced combined ratio by 20% and increased written premium by 33%.

Achieved these results through . . .

- refocusing underwriting and marketing efforts on target market segments, larger accounts and unique coverages, i.e., the electronics industry, large highway and heavy construction, agency underwritten small accounts, condominiums and inland marine classes

June 1983–July 1986: Industry Underwriting Officer-Director
Commercial Insurance Division, Corporate Headquarters

Responsible for research and development, implementation and management of insurance programs for targeted industry groups, specifically electronics and construction.

Results

- Developed $60 million in premium with a combined ratio under 95% by creating and managing the electronics industry underwriting program, recognized as one of the two premier programs of its kind in the insurance industry.
- Created and managed the computer services and software errors and omissions coverage, a product that rapidly became the industry standard; produced $12 million in premium in three years with a loss ratio under 30%.

Achieved these results through managing . . .

- research, development and implementation efforts associated with this new industry group
- design and implementation of the headquarters, region and service center field underwriting and marketing organization
- group programs in the electronics and construction industries, including programs for the two largest electronics industry trade associations
- training seminars for service center underwriters, agents, brokers and insurance buyers

February 1981–June 1983: Package Underwriting Department Manager
Washington, D.C. Area Service Center, Fairfax, VA

Responsible for underwriting commercial property, general liability, umbrella, automobile, workers' compensation, fidelity bond and medical malpractice insurance. Managed a staff of twenty-four and a written premium of $15 million.

Results

- Turned around an unprofitable department with declining premium volume.
- Reduced the combined ratio by 15%; increased written premium by 30%.

April 1976–February 1981: Property Underwriting Department Manager
Washington, D.C. Area Service Center, Fairfax, VA

Responsible for commercial property and inland marine, residential fire, personal inland marine and homeowners insurance. Managed a staff of sixteen and $10 million of written premium.

Results
- Achieved combined ratios under 85% and increased written premium over 400%.

October 1973–April 1976: Commercial Property Underwriter
Washington, D.C. Area Service Center, Fairfax, VA

April 1973–October 1973: Property Underwriting Trainee
East Orange Service Center, East Orange, NJ

Education
- University of Minnesota, B.A., 1972; majors in political science and sociology
- Insurance Institute of America, Associate in Risk Management and Certificate in General Principles of Insurance
- Chartered Property and Casualty Underwriter, CPCU, five parts

Other Interests
- scuba diving
- skiing
- golf
- politics
- community affairs

David P. Kaiser

**873 Wooster Lane
Memphis, TN 38116
901-688-7022, home; 901-854-4880, office
901-4677, FAX**

After

David P. Kaiser
873 Wooster Lane
Memphis, TN 38116
H: 901-688-7022
W: 901-854-4880
FAX: 901-854-4677

OBJECTIVE
Vice President of Commercial Underwriting for USF&G

SUMMARY
Experience includes developing and managing new programs and products, achieving a return on equity in excess of 15% and annual written premium of $3 million to $60 million for each of these target markets:

- Computer services and software
- Educational institutions
- Financial services
- High technology manufacturers
- Hospitality, recreation and leisure

- Limousine operators
- Medical equipment manufacturers
- Museums
- Oil field services
- Social services

EMPLOYMENT HISTORY

1973–1992 St. Paul Fire and Marine Insurance Company
A property and liability insurance company with annual premium of $3 billion, a member of The St. Paul Companies, a worldwide insurance organization.

May 1988 to March 1992 Senior Underwriting Officer
Commercial Insurance Division, Corporate Headquarters
Head of the Business Development Department, responsible for $750 million in written premium, approximately 25% of the company's total. Managed a staff of 12 and a budget of $1.3 million.

- Increased annual premium in target markets from $48 million to $175 million by creating and managing new target market programs and coverages.
- Produced an estimated ultimate loss ratio under 50% with a resulting return on equity of over 15%.

July 1986 to May 1988 Commercial Insurance Underwriting Manager
New England Service Center, Springfield, MA
Managed the commercial insurance underwriting department: a staff of 36 in two offices; $60 million in premium; a six-state territory.

David P. Kaiser   Page 2

- Turned around an operation that was unprofitable with declining premium volume.
- Reduced combined ratio by 20% and increased written premium by 33%.
- Refocused underwriting and marketing efforts on target market segments, larger accounts and unique coverages.

June 1983 to July 1986 Industry Underwriting Officer-Director
Commercial Insurance Division, Corporate Headquarters
Responsible for research and development and management of insurance programs for targeted industry groups, specifically electronics and construction.

- Developed $60 million in premium with a combined ratio under 95% by creating and managing the electronics industry underwriting program, recognized as one of the two premier programs of its kind in the insurance industry.
- Created and managed the computer services and software errors and omissions coverage, a product that rapidly became the industry standard; produced $12 million in premium in three years with a loss ratio under 30%.

February 1981 to June 1983 Package Underwriting Department Manager
Washington, DC, Area Service Center, Fairfax, VA
Responsible for underwriting commercial property, general liability, umbrella, automobile, workers' compensation, fidelity bond and medical malpractice insurance. Managed a staff of 24 and a written premium of $15 million.

- Turned around an unprofitable department with declining premium volume.
- Reduced the combined ratio by 15%; increased written premium by 30%.

April 1976 to February 1981 Property Underwriting Department Manager
Washington, DC, Area Service Center
Responsible for commercial property and inland marine, residential fire, personal inland marine and homeowners insurance. Managed a staff of 16 and $10 million of written premium.

- Achieved combined ratios under 85% and increased written premium over 400%.

EDUCATION
- Chartered Property and Casualty Underwriter, CPCU, five parts
- Insurance Institute of America, Associate in Risk Management and Certificate in General Principles of Insurance
- BA, University of Minnesota

OTHER INTERESTS
- Scuba diving
- Skiing
- Golf
- Politics
- Community affairs

Success Stories

The resumes in this book represent real people. Some of them have interesting stories that they're willing to share. Here are a few.

Diane Hill

Diane Hill is an experienced executive secretary who prides herself on being able to work independently, anticipate a manager's needs, interact with people at all levels of an organization and translate and transcribe complicated technical jargon. Everyone who knows Diane would describe her as a role model for an ideal assistant.

Unfortunately, even "water walkers" can be terminated in company downsizings. When Dallas Area Rapid Transit, Diane's employer, reduced its staff, she found herself looking for another position. To turn lemons into lemonade, she decided to get a fresh start in a new city.

When her outplacement counselor heard about Diane's plans to relocate, she called a colleague in Atlanta to inquire about the job market there for executive secretaries. She also arranged for Diane to meet an Atlanta career planner who could provide important contacts.

Diane found an apartment during a reconnoitering trip, then headed for Atlanta with her daughter during the holidays. After taking a few weeks to get settled, she started accepting temporary assignments to get a feel for available positions. After a few months, she was offered a permanent job as the administrative assistant for the Dean of the School of Business at Clark Atlanta University, where she continues to enjoy the academic atmosphere and the interaction with the students.

Diane C. Hill
2960 Duncan Avenue
Atlanta, GA 30367
404-387-6999

OBJECTIVE

Administrative Assistant to the Dean of the School of Business, Clark Atlanta University

PERSONAL QUALIFICATIONS

- Fifteen years of secretarial experience.
- Accustomed to working with Board of Directors, executive and senior level management.
- Accomplished at taking minutes and interpreting technical language to produce understandable reports.
- Work extremely well under pressure and with very little supervision.

EXPERIENCE

Dallas Area Rapid Transit (DART)   **Dallas, Texas**   **1986–1992**
Senior Administrative Secretary
to Assistant Executive Director (AED) for Planning

- Serve as administrative resource and personal secretary for above executive.
- Assist AED with daily operations of the Planning Department.
- Often serve as AED's liaison to Board of Directors, Planning Department staff, community and municipal leaders.
- Attend and transcribe minutes of the DART Board Planning Committee.
- Coordinate office activities of five division secretaries.
- Handle confidential personnel matters.
- Perform general secretarial duties.

Senior Administrative Secretary
to Assistant Executive Director for Consumer Affairs
and Assistant Executive Director for Real Estate

- Assisted AEDs in managing Consumer Affairs and Real Estate divisions in a start-up organization.
- Attended and transcribed minutes of DART Board Minority Affairs Committee.
- Coordinated hiring activities for two departments.
- Composed correspondence, processed expense reports, and made travel arrangements.
- Responsible for executives' schedules and appointments.
- Performed general secretarial duties.

Diane C. Hill   Page 2

ARCO Oil and Gas Company   **Dallas, Texas**   **1981–1985**
Senior Secretary to Company Medical Director
- Served as office manager for the director's office and clinic.
- Processed disability and retirement applications.
- Gathered confidential medical information for Medical Director.
- Scheduled executive medical appointments.
- Used dictaphone extensively in transcription work.

Senior Secretary to Budget Group Manager
- Assisted Manager in daily operations of the department.
- Coordinated logistics of ARCO Annual Budget Conference.
- Frequently interacted with district and senior management.
- Handled confidential personnel matters.

Secretary to Budget Group Directors
- Reported to two Directors and performed general secretarial duties for their staff.
- Duties required heavy statistical typing.
- Maintained central filing system.
- Served as backup for Senior Secretary.

American Express Company   **Dallas, Texas**   **1979–1980**
Senior Secretary to Regional Vice President
- Handled territorial sales tracking for VP's office.
- Assisted in customer service problem solving.
- Processed expense reports, did light bookkeeping, made travel arrangements and coordinated executive calendar.

Advertising Research Foundation   **New York, New York**   **1978**
Secretary to Senior Research Associate and Marketing Director
- Processed research data for public relations, marketing, and research agencies.
- Assisted Marketing Director in coordinating company's Annual Research Fair.
- Processed information for new members of the Foundation.

EDUCATION   1967–1977   Katharine Gibbs School
                                  New York, New York
                   1972–1973   Newark State College
                                  Union, New Jersey

TRAINING   WordPerfect 5.1 and MicroSoft Word 5.0
                   IBM Personal Computer, Xerox 860 Word Processor
                   Lanier Word Processor

Marilyn Hamen

Marilyn moved from Florida when her husband's company transferred him to a new position in Texas. Like Diane, she has exceptional skills in her profession, and she is the type of employee any school district would be delighted to hire.

To find a teaching position where she could use her advanced skills and work with a principal who offers staff members considerable latitude, Marilyn developed a master plan for her job search that included three key elements:

1. A resume emphasizing her initiative and reading expertise.
2. Networking appointments with principals of the elementary schools within a 20-minute radius of her home.
3. Investigation of the certification process in her new state.

Shortly after starting her search, she was offered a position in the school of her choice. She reports that her first year in her new job has been the best in 12 years of teaching.

MARILYN HAMEN
26 Bishop Avenue
Granada Hills, TX 76032
817-625-3221

OBJECTIVE

Primary teacher for the Hurst-Euless-Bedford Independent School District, where expertise in reading techniques would be particularly useful.

WORK EXPERIENCE

Kindergarten and First Grade Teacher, Woodland Elementary, Pasco County School District, 1981–1992

One of three teachers from Woodland (65 teachers) who attended the State Education Enhancement Institute. As a result of this training, developed and implemented a schoolwide positive self-esteem program called W.O.W. Set goals, brainstormed activities, presented ideas to faculty, motivated teachers and students to get involved every week. Evaluated and refined program based on teacher, student and parent feedback.

Served as Grade Chairperson for six years.

Developed and presented a theme approach seminar at the Florida State Reading Conference and County Whole Language Workshop.

Consistently elected as a school representative for district inservices. Presented school-based teacher training programs developed from these in service curricula.

Certified as a Gesell Developmental Screener, which recognizes expertise in placing children in developmentally appropriate learning environments.

Pioneered whole language and literature-based techniques in both kindergarten and first grade.

Recipient of the Associate Master Teacher Certification from the State of Florida, the highest designation in Florida's merit teacher program.

Migrant Reading Teacher, Pasco Elementary, Pasco County School District, 1979–1981

Supervised a staff of seven paraprofessionals who tutored up to 140 migrant students per year in reading. Provided training in reading techniques and materials to these tutors.

Compiled and maintained MSRTS (Migrant Student Record Transfer System) records to be used in a nationwide data base.

Marilyn Hamen   Page 2

 Served as a liaison for the program with the classroom teachers.
 Scheduled tutoring and kept teachers informed of student progress.

 Taught ESL to a selected group of first-grade students.

Kindergarten Teacher, Iola Roberts Elementary, St. Clair County Schools, Pell City, Alabama, 1978–1979

 Selected as one of the first 10 kindergarten teachers in the county. Team taught with another teacher.

Third Grade Teacher, West Zephyrhills Elementary, Pasco County School District, 1973–1975

 Taught third grade in a year-round school system.

EDUCATION

 MA, Reading Education, University of South Florida, Tampa, Florida, 1980
 BA, Education, Stetson University, Deland, Florida, 1973
 Completed training for SACS team evaluator
 IRA Conference, 4 years
 FRA Conference, 10 years
 SACUS Conferences, 3 years
 At least 400 in-service hours on a variety of educational issues and techniques

PROFESSIONAL ASSOCIATIONS

 Member, IRA, FRA and Pasco County Reading Council
 Member, SACUS
 AΔK Women Educators' Honorary, held a variety of offices

Videotape of developmental writing lesson for kindergarten available for viewing.

Other Good Chronological Resumes

Because so many people sent in excellent examples of chronological resumes, here are some others representing a variety of careers and industries. Feel free to use them as models, but be careful about resorting to a fill-in-the-blank approach. The main reason these resumes stand out from hundreds of others is that they contain a compelling message about individual achievements. For your resume to be equally powerful, it must be uniquely yours.

EDWARD JENNINGS   10555 South Grand
                                                           Big Bend, AZ 85044
                                                           602-666-3804

OBJECTIVE   A career position in marketing or strategic planning
                      Special Interest—High Tech

QUALIFICATIONS   ◆ 8 years international marketing management experience
                      ◆ Expertise in strategic planning for mature and new products
                      ◆ Specialization in product positioning, definition, development &
                         expansion
                      ◆ Background in opening, developing and expanding markets
                      ◆ Strong communication, motivation, team building, liaison and leadership
                      ◆ Masters in International Marketing & Bachelors in Computer Science

PROFESSIONAL   **Strategic Planning & Marketing Manager**
EXPERIENCE   Intel Connectivity Division   Chandler AZ   1984–1994
                      ◆ Directed strategic planning for new product development and start-up
                         operations, new market introduction for retail branded products and
                         semiconductor line including product definition, product enhancements,
                         target and niche marketing strategies and product introduction strategies
                      ◆ Developed guidelines, negotiations and training for $6M spent on
                         strategic partnerships
                      ◆ Successfully wrote funding proposals for new product development
                      ◆ Hired, trained and developed marketing professionals

                      Senior Product Marketing Engineer
                      Intel Corporation   Chandler AZ
                      ◆ Managed product marketing operations including strategic marketing
                         and product planning for 30 million unit product line with 45%
                         product margin
                      ◆ Developed product pricing strategies, demand forecasts,
                         merchandizing programs and business development plans
                      ◆ Devised operational support infrastructure for product line including
                         technical training and field sales training, contract guidelines and
                         product support documentation

                      Customer Marketing Engineer
                      Intel Corporation   Chandler AZ
                      ◆ Managed sales administration & factory support for external sales
                         engineers—clients were Honeywell, Xerox, Westinghouse, Sperry & ISG
                      ◆ Developed forecasting strategies and implemented streamlined
                         procedures for contract approvals and quote procedures
                      ◆ Devised operational support infrastructure for product line including
                         technical training and field sales training, contract guidelines and
                         product support documentation
                      ◆ Generated business plans, reviews, account profiles and built expansion
                         strategies resulting in a 40% increase in the Honeywell business

Regional Lodging Specialist
NCR Corporation   Pittsburgh PA   1979–1983
♦ Introduced a new product line to hotel industry
♦ Coordinated competitive analysis projects & developed technical seminars
♦ Exceeded sales quota by 147%

Account Manager
NCR Corporation   Pittsburgh PA
♦ Managed sales of computer hardware, software and point-of-sale equipment
♦ Utilized cost-benefit analysis sales techniques and customized presentations
♦ Improved sales to 809% of quota

EDUCATION   **Masters in International Marketing**   1984
American Graduate School of International Management—Thunderbird

Bachelors of Science in Computer Science   1981
Point Park College   Pittsburgh PA

Bachelors of Science in Administration   1978
Duquesne University   Pittsburgh PA

Management Training
♦ Effective Communications—Written & Oral
♦ Project Management & Professional Team Building
♦ Win-Win Contract Negotiations

Professional Training
♦ International Business Practices
♦ High Tech Brand Management
♦ Value Based Pricing

Technical Training
♦ Wired & Wireless Wide Area Network Connectivity
♦ Portable Personal Computers
♦ Computer Peripheral Equipment
♦ Microcontrollers

LEADERSHIP   ♦ Toastmasters International
♦ US Wado Karate-Do Federation
♦ Private Pilots License

HONORS   ♦ Outstanding Expansion & Profitability Award   1992
♦ Advertising Age Magazine Award   1991
♦ Outstanding Performance for Worldwide Design Wins 1989

JEFFREY H. BRAND
8 Better Drive
Lake Forest, IL 60658
312-373-9686

OBJECTIVE   Position with a real estate development or management firm in commercial leasing or acquisitions.

EXPERIENCE

Leasing Representative, Pyramid Companies, Syracuse, NY   1990
  - Leased space to retail tenants in 16 regional shopping malls.
  - Personally responsible for leasing a newly constructed 685,000-square-foot mall in eastern Massachusetts.
  - Prospected and developed regional and local accounts.
  - Analyzed viability of prospective tenant business plans.

Leasing Representative, Picerne Properties, Providence, RI   1989–90
  - Managed a 1.5 million-square-foot commercial portfolio of both existing and development projects in partnership with another representative.
  - Achieved yearly quota in six months.
  - Prospected and secured leases with national accounts such as Computerland, BoRics, and Strawberry Records.

Manager, Venture Realty Associates, Boston, MA   1987–89
  - Managed and marketed newly acquired warehouse and office properties.
  - Conducted acquisition analyses for commercial and industrial properties including office buildings, parking lots, and warehouses.
  - Negotiated leases for retail food stores with national mall developers.
  - Supervised construction of several projects from initial blueprints to completion.

Rental Agent, Universal Brokerage Services and Back Bay Realty, Boston, MA
                                                                        1986–1987
                (Held full-time job while attending school)
  - Assisted in establishing new rental division.
  - Prospected and obtained new property listings and maintained relationships with existing clients.
  - Developed advertising strategy.
  - Executed leases.

EDUCATION   BS/BA Boston University, Boston, MA, Marketing Major, 1987

LICENSES   Massachusetts Real Estate Brokers license

COLLEGE   Member Sigma Alpha Epsilon Fraternity
ACTIVITIES   Boston University Sailing Team
             Boston University Men's Lacrosse Team

INTERESTS   Architecture, Spanish, Sailing, Swimming, Mountain Biking, Squash

WILLIAM C. MICHALAK
14630 N. Canard Lane
Chicago, IL 60620
312-305-5614
312-777-6236

OBJECTIVE

Vice President of Human Resources.

CAREER SUMMARY

Fifteen years of Human Resources experience including department management, policy writing, staffing, AAP/EEO, counseling, training and development, compensation/benefits, HR database development and implementation. Extensive work in management development, succession planning and linking human resource activities to the business plan.

PROFESSIONAL SUMMARY

Since 1991   **Amoco Production Company,** General Office   Chicago, IL
Consultant, Human Resources Planning & Development

Succession planning and management development responsibility, focusing on top 130 positions, replacement candidates, and high-potential employees. Significant accomplishments include:

- Resurrecting the succession planning process after a two-year moratorium, leading to senior management's understanding and effective use of human resource planning systems throughout the organization as a source of competitive advantage.
- Providing leadership and technical support for a global cultural diversity initiative, focusing management's attention on the strategic imperatives around diversity, and developing a process to help in achieving the desired results.

1987–1991   **Amoco Corporation,** Corporate Headquarters   Chicago, IL
Consultant, Management Development

Responsible for succession planning and management development with a focus on the top 60 positions, replacement candidates and high potential employees. Significant accomplishments:

- Designed, developed and implemented a succession process to focus attention on executive management replacement and development.
- Consulted with operating companies on a replacement planning and management development process to include middle management levels.
- Supported an executive development program targeting the top 100 executives and a corporate university targeting the top 3,000 managers.
- Provided leadership and support to a task force of senior line managers that resulted in a new companywide performance management process.

1983–1987   **Borg-Warner Corporation,** Corporate Headquarters   Chicago, IL
Corporate Manager, Human Resource Development

Responsible for succession planning/management development processes with a focus on corporate and subsidiary officer level positions (150 executives from a population of 88,000).

Significant accomplishments:
- Refined and institutionalized succession planning/management development system in a highly decentralized environment leading to a better strategic fit between executives, replacement candidates, executive development and the business plans.
- Refined and administered individually focused assessment and development workshop aimed at high-potential middle managers. Evaluated their management/leadership style and versatility in dealing with situations typical of general management or senior level staff positions.

1976–1983   **Borg-Warner Financial Services, Inc.**   Chicago, IL

Compensation Manager (1983)

Compensation responsibility for salary administration, analysis of competitor and industry pay practices and recommendation of pay policy. Significant accomplishments:
- Designed, developed and implemented a revised manager bonus program with front-end input by incumbents and a direct link to performance.
- Developed and designed a performance appraisal system, emphasizing individual contributions and accountabilities with direct linkage to the job evaluation system, resulting in clarification of performance expectations.

Manager Employee Relations (1980–1982)

Managed human resource department providing support to a 300-branch office, multinational operation. Responsible for clerical staffing, benefits administration, policy development and implementation, career/personal counseling, APP/EEO, program planning and automation of department. Significant accomplishments included:
- Enhanced stature of the department from maintenance type personnel function to a visible, proactive, human resource function.
- Automated HR database, AAP reporting and unemployment claim reporting.

EDUCATION
University of Chicago, Chicago, Illinois
Various graduate level courses through Returning Scholar Program

St. Joseph's Calumet College, Whiting, Indiana
BA Psychology, 1976

PROFESSIONAL & COMMUNITY AFFILIATIONS

St. Coletta's School and Training Center	Chairman of the Board
Catholic Charities	Advisory Board Member
Human Resource Planning Society	Member
Human Resource Management Association of Chicago	Member

"Thanks for the offer, but I really don't want to work here . . . I just wanted a second opinion on my resume."

6

Functional Resumes

Functional resumes are the "new kids on the block." Instead of highlighting experience by job title, they group accomplishments by functional area or overall job objective. The following sections show examples of these two approaches.

Experience by Functional Area

BUSINESS DEVELOPMENT/SALES
  • Developed and managed $13 million loan portfolio for 175 customers composed of corporate executives, doctors, attorneys, CPAs, wealthy individuals, and private companies.

- Built a $3 million life insurance practice in 1½ years serving 100 upper-income clients.
- Recruited, trained and developed a unit of five life insurance agents producing over $5 million in insurance sales in a 12-month period.
- Planned and implemented new business development program for S&L branch; awarded President's Trophy for top production.

COMMUNITY INVOLVEMENT

- Served on Board of Urban Services for the YMCA and as Division Leader of Annual Campaign, 1989.
- Active on Board of the Way Back House and on its fund-raising committee.
- Participated as Administrative Board member and teacher, Highland Park Methodist Church.
- Contributed many hours as coach and leader for YMCA Youth Sports and Indian Guides.
- Active Dallas native with numerous contacts developed in civic, business and educational sectors.

Experience by Job Objective

EXPERIENCE HIGHLIGHTS

- Managed the development and sale of a wide range of highly profitable financial and computer-based services to thousands of corporations and financial institutions worldwide.
- As Senior Vice President and Deputy Department Head of the International Division of EurAm Bank, directed and administered its lending operations in Europe, the Asia/Pacific region, and Africa.
- Played a major role in opening the London branch of the bank.
- Cultivated relationships with companies and financial institutions in the London market.
- Served as liaison with the Head Office in New York.
- Established the branch's Credit Department.
- Coordinated facilities preparations from working with the architects to choosing the chef.
- Spearheaded and supervised the largest syndicated loan in EurAm history.
- Planned and conducted a road show for potential U.S. lenders featuring presentations by the borrowing country's Finance Ministry, Central Bank, and Treasury.
- Pioneered a new loan pricing concept aimed at attracting regional banks into the syndicate.
- Cultivated continuing relationships with high-level contacts in commercial and central banks, government agencies, and corporations all over the world, particularly in Europe.

Aside from not listing experience by job title, the functional resume differs from the chronological one by rarely using dates of employment or an employment history. Job titles and company names may appear in the text of the achievement per se, but they do not dictate the structure of the Experience section. For instance, an accomplishment in a functional resume may be described in the following style:

- Managed the production of seven brochures, four 10-minute videotapes, and a variety of PSAs and press releases as Director of Community Relations for the Metropolitan YMCA.

As with any format, the functional resume has its good and bad points. Review them to see whether they apply to your situation.

The Pros

This approach to resume writing is an excellent vehicle for putting together paid and nonpaid experience without the confusion of conflicting dates and titles. It's particularly useful when volunteer assignments or life experience support your job objective more effectively than your paid work. It assumes that your performance of a task had value even if you weren't paid for doing it.

It allows you to place your most relevant experience at the top of your resume, even if it's several years old. This feature is especially useful if your career has veered off its intended path, or a new direction hasn't met your expectations.

The functional resume doesn't focus on dates. Consequently, job gaps, job-hopping and staying too long in one place aren't issues for concern.

For career changers, who need to concentrate on functional rather than specialized skills, this format emphasizes what they can do rather than where they did it. Example: "Devising a system to increase customer contact by 50%" is a worthy accomplishment wherever you achieve it. Attaching it to a particular company or industry isn't as important as the fact that you know how to do it.

The Cons

Many people don't like functional resumes. Unfortunately, these individuals often are important to your search. They include personnel recruiters, executive search professionals and technical managers. They screen candidates for many openings that might interest you and become nervous when they don't see dates and job titles in reverse chronological order. They tend to think functional resume writers have something to hide. If you send a functional resume to one of them, you risk being rejected. On the other hand, if this approach tells your story effectively, don't abandon it in favor of a more traditional, chronological format, which will likely focus on the very things you want to minimize.

Another problem may be that you're uncomfortable with this style. A cardinal rule of resume writing is to produce a document that represents you personally. If you don't buy this approach, don't use it. Only a believer should play with the new kid on the block.

For individuals who are not adept at synthesizing data into functional categories, this format can be a real challenge. While it's relatively easy to list achievements by job title, it takes a little more creativity to group them into clusters of activities. If you are having difficulty visualizing what some typical functions might be, refer to the resumes in this chapter or start with the following categories:

Production Planning	Project Management	Public Speaking
Training	Financial Management	Event Planning
Sales/Marketing	Consulting	Troubleshooting
Customer Service	Administration	Inventory Control
Fund Raising	Quality Management	Human Resources
International Business	Public Relations	Leadership

Don't assume that this list includes every function you should mention. Rather, it represents only a few of the myriad types of tasks that many professionals perform daily.

Before-and-After Example

Bob Barrett

Bob Barrett is a business generalist with many years of experience in the energy business. When the oil and gas industry hit bottom in the 1980s, he decided to accept a sweetened severance package and seek a new career. Bob wanted a resume that would spotlight his project management and troubleshooting experience, without labeling him as an oil man. In his first attempt, which follows, several areas need improvement. His job objective is too broad. He either needs to develop a specific target or leave off the objective altogether.

While he listed his experience by job title, he didn't complete the thought by including dates as well. A resume reader who sees a job title immediately looks for corresponding dates. If you want to delete dates, don't use job titles.

Like many job seekers, he described his job duties instead of how he performed them. Some specific quantifiable achievements would give his resume a lot more punch.

Before

ROBERT L. BARRETT
27 Ridge Road
Omaha, NE 68127
402-683-1122

OBJECTIVE

Energy-related Marketing, Supply, or Staff Position.

BACKGROUND

Comprehensive knowledge of petroleum industry with particular expertise in natural gas liquids business practices. Progressively responsible marketing and administrative positions with a major integrated energy company.

PROFESSIONAL EXPERIENCE

SUN COMPANY, INC.

Manager, Bulk Sales and Pricing

Developed and managed propane bulk sales strategy. Negotiated spot sales and bulk sales contracts with other producers, multistate marketers and large independent marketers. Monitored spot markets and revised sales plans. Coordinated competitive price analyses and recommended price changes.

— Planned and implemented a major bulk sales program resulting in diversified sales channels and increased return on surplus inventory sales.
— Developed professional rapport and solidified business relationships with representatives of major accounts.
— Acted as company representative for providing market and price information to industry publications and pricing services.

Manager, NGL Marketing Operations

Organized and managed support unit for the consolidated operations of NGL Supply and Logistics and Wholesale Propane Marketing departments. Responsibilities included customer service; contract administration; sales and supply analysis and forecasting; expense processing and control; pricing administration; liaison with field offices; business policy development.

— Directed successful project to computerize natural gas liquids contract preparation and provide on-line contract information for reporting and analysis.
— Structured comprehensive management financial statement to analyze business line profitability within NGL Marketing Division.
— Developed key-stop truck loading authorization and insurance certification procedure for NGL terminals to provide security and risk management compliance.

ROBERT L. BARRETT

Manager, Special Projects & Administration

Managed natural gas liquids administrative processes. Conducted complex problem-solving projects and provided ongoing consultative expertise to NGL Supply and Logistics department regarding business processes and procedures.

— Developed standard form natural gas liquids contracts, contract administration processes, and trained supply and sales personnel in contract preparation.
— Directed industry compensation survey for NGL supply and sales professionals.
— Recommended and implemented procedures between natural gas liquids and accounting, credit and legal departments.
— Developed and implemented product exchange policy and controls.

Manager, NGL Operational Administration

Directed NGL supply and distribution operational services including staff support, product scheduling, forecasting, budget preparation and long-range plan development. Managed professional and clerical employees.

— Devised new organizational structure and strategy to accommodate expanded natural gas liquids business.
— Led staffing effort including job description development and selection of representatives for expanded organization.
— Developed interface procedures between NGL Supply and Distribution and production, refining and LPG Marketing units.
— Designated as Division Representative on company Job Evaluation Committee (Hay Method).

NGL Office Supervisor

Supervised development of product forecasts, inventory projections, budgets, and scheduling of truck, rail, and pipeline shipments. Performed contract administration and supervised office staff.

Prior Assignments

— Natural Gas Liquids Analyst
— Division Order Analyst
— Crude Oil Supply & Transportation Trainee

EDUCATION   BS—Business Administration—Marketing Major
Oklahoma State University

To improve his resume, Bob decided to omit his objective until he could develop a specific one based on an ad, networking appointment or other source. He changed his Background section, which focused on the energy industry, to a Personal Qualifications that summarizes his business generalist and project management skills. Under Experience Highlights, he took out the job titles and replaced them with accomplishments. To give a better feel for the scope of his activities, he used a lot of quantification and included the names of key commercial accounts that would be recognizable to most people. He also included a shortened work history at the bottom of his resume along with a number of years for each position.

After

ROBERT L. BARRETT
27 Ridge Road
Omaha, NE 68127
402-683-1122

PERSONAL QUALIFICATIONS

— Business generalist with record of achievement in applying marketing, administrative and human resources skills to effectively manage both projects and ongoing operations.

— Multiple years of experience including selling, supervision and special assignments in "front-line" business activities.

— Rapport builder with interpersonal abilities demonstrated in both internal and external business situations.

— Adept at addressing work processes and new systems, and coordinating task force projects.

— Regard integrity, stability and professionalism as critical components of my business philosophy.

EXPERIENCE HIGHLIGHTS

— Developed and managed strategy for sales of a major product generating annual revenue of $9,500,000.

  — Negotiated sales contracts and cultivated business relationships with major commercial accounts (such as Texaco, Occidental Petroleum, Farmland Industries and Land O'Lakes).

  — Coordinated competitive price analyses and recommended price changes.

  — Acted as company representative for providing market and price information to industry publications and pricing services.

  — Spearheaded development of a computerized customer telephone notification system to offset manpower reductions.

— Managed support activities for a major marketing unit. Supervised customer service, contract administration, sales analysis and forecasting, expense processing and control, administrative procedures, liaison with field offices and business policy development.

  — Consolidated the support operations of two marketing units, reducing staff by 50%.

  — Developed customer truck-loading authorization and insurance certification procedures for marketing terminals to provide security and risk management compliance.

— Developed standard form contracts, contract administration processes, and trained sales and supply personnel in contract preparation.

ROBERT L. BARRETT   **Page Two**

— Directed the computerization of marketing contract preparation and contract information systems, saving 650 personnel hours per month.
— Managed development and analysis of a $350,000,000 departmental operating budget.
— Designed financial statement to separate and analyze revenue, costs, and profitability for three business lines generating the above revenue.
— Devised new organizational structure and strategy to accommodate business expansion. Put together job descriptions and professional staff for expanded organization.
— Directed industry compensation survey for supply and sales professionals.
— Coordinated geographical relocation of a department. Selected and trained new support personnel.
— Designated as Marketing Division representative on Company Procedures and Job Evaluation Committees (Hay Method).

WORK HISTORY—SUN COMPANY, INC.
— Manager, Marketing Operations—4 years
— Manager, Bulk Sales and Pricing—2 years
— Manager, Operational Administration—3 years
— Manager, Special Projects—4 years

Previous Assignments
— Office Supervisor
— Purchases and Sales Analyst
— Administrative Trainee

EDUCATION
BS—Business Administration-Marketing Major, Oklahoma State University

Success Stories

Brenda Barrett

Brenda had been Director of Operations for her family's insurance business for several years. Because she majored in psychology and had an ongoing interest in that area, she spent a lot of personal time doing volunteer work in crisis intervention. Eventually her commitment to helping people led to her leave the family business and move into nonprofit management. As she was concerned about the difficulty of marketing her business experience in a nonprofit setting, she decided to use a functional format to spotlight her volunteer work and describe her job activities by type of task rather than by job title.

Two of Brenda's resumes created for nonprofit openings follow. Note how Brenda draws from her background and uses the same experience to tailor two different resumes. To gain the maximum results from your resumes, you should adopt this approach as well.

P.S. Brenda got the job at the Dallas Hospice, then left after a few years to move back into the business world. She's currently Assistant to the Chief Council for International Business at Oryx Energy Corporation in Dallas.

BRENDA BARRETT   32 Meadow Drive
214-938-2403   Dallas, TX 75243

OBJECTIVE   Business manager for the Routh Street Clinic where I hope to use
my management background and crisis intervention skills.

PERSONAL QUALIFICATIONS

- Four years' experience in managing a service business with $3.5 million volume.
- A long-standing personal commitment to a woman's right to control her own body.
- A solid record of volunteer achievement in crisis intervention, counseling, and teaching.

APPLICABLE EXPERIENCE

BUSINESS MANAGEMENT

- Developed and implemented operations systems for three general agencies and a premium financial company, subsidiaries of Barrett & Associates, Inc.
- Projected our image and developed professional rapport with agents around the state while keeping them abreast of company policies and procedures.
- Evaluated potential and active trouble spots involving staff, customers, and companies; reported findings and recommendations to management; resolved problems and revised existing systems.
- Monitored legal, governmental and cultural changes that might affect the insurance and premium finance industries and suggested necessary modifications to ensure compliance.
- Hired, trained and supervised a staff of four people.
- Reestablished customer trust on previously underserviced accounts.
- Researched and purchased the best available deals in supplies and capital fixtures.

COUNSELING AND CRISIS INTERVENTION

- Counseled over 700 persons using the crisis intervention model while volunteering once a week for the Suicide and Crisis Center.
- Cofacilitated the volunteer training program for the Center, which included the theory and practice of crisis intervention, the profile of the person in crisis, active listening skills, role playing, team building and the fostering of personal growth.
- Acted as a role model for new trainees getting on-the-job training.

EDUCATION   1986   BS in Psychology, UTD

Over 20 hours of continuing education in crisis intervention theory and application. The Road Less Traveled, a personal discovery, goal-setting workshop.

BRENDA BARRETT
32 Meadow Drive
Dallas, Texas 75243
214-938-2403

OBJECTIVE   Volunteer Director for Dallas Hospice Center, Inc., where I hope to use my administrative background and crisis intervention skills.

PERSONAL QUALIFICATIONS
- A long-standing personal commitment to the right to die with dignity.
- A solid record of volunteer achievement in crisis intervention, counseling, and teaching.
- Four years' experience in managing a service business with $3.5 million volume.

APPLICABLE EXPERIENCE

Volunteer Management and Counseling Skills
- Cofacilitated the volunteer training program for the Suicide and Crisis Center, which included the theory and practice of crisis intervention, the profile of the person in crisis, active listening skills, role playing, team building and the fostering of personal growth.
- Recruited, trained and supervised a team of 25 people.
- Acted as a role model for new trainees getting on-the-job training.
- Counseled over 700 persons using the crisis intervention model while volunteering once a week for the Suicide and Crisis Center.
- Counseled bereaved families who had recently experienced the death of a hospice patient.

Public Relations and Development
- Projected our image and developed professional rapport with 300 agents around the state while keeping them abreast of company policies and procedures.
- Developed a premium finance package and presented it to over 100 companies in two states.
- Reestablished customer trust on previously underserviced accounts.
- Served on Speaker's Bureau for Suicide and Crisis Center.

Business Management
- Developed and implemented operations systems for three general agencies and a premium financial company, subsidiaries of Barrett & Associates, Inc.
- Evaluated potential and active trouble spots involving staff, customers and companies; reported findings and recommendations to management; resolved problems and revised existing systems.
- Monitored legal, governmental and cultural changes that might affect the insurance and premium finance industries and suggested necessary modifications to ensure compliance.

EDUCATION   1986 BS in Psychology, UTD

Over 20 hours of continuing education in crisis intervention theory and application. The Road Less Traveled, a personal discovery, goal-setting workshop.

Liz Wally

As a professional volunteer for 15 years, Liz served on many Boards of Directors, chairing numerous committees, spearheading new organizations and raising thousands of dollars. Eventually, she became an unpaid consultant to a variety of nonprofit organizations. When her children started college, she decided to parlay her volunteer expertise into a paid position.

Liz's first foray into the for-profit arena was to start a group for singles called Grapevine, where intelligent people could interact through spirited discussions similar to college bull sessions. She reasoned that many people were uncomfortable with dating and would prefer to meet and get to know each other during the Grapevine's opinion exchanges.

Eventually, Liz decided that Grapevine was more of a hobby than a business, and she began to seek other alternatives. Her first taste of conflict resolution occurred when she attended a seminar on the subject at the Women's Peace Conference. She was so intrigued by conflict resolution techniques and their potential applications in a variety of settings that she decided to learn the process in depth.

After receiving extensive training and doing volunteer work for a local Dispute Mediation Service, Liz developed a program to teach conflict resolution to adults and children in the metropolitan school district. Last year, her program served 68 schools in 4 districts. She is now a paid consultant for the Dallas Dispute Mediation Service, Inc., and has added three people to her staff to handle the demand for her burgeoning program. Note how her resume—designed to mirror her ideal job description—fits beautifully with the career she has chosen.

LIZ WALLY
3320 Kaiser Boulevard
Dallas, TX 75268
214-249-7166

OBJECTIVE   Project management in an entrepreneurial organization where initiating new programs or changes, visualizing the big picture, creative problem solving, organizing tasks, ideas and people and monitoring follow-through are prerequisites.

QUALIFICATIONS

- Fifteen years of executive and Board experience with diverse nonprofit organizations.
- Founder of several professional and civic groups geared to meet specific community needs.
- Coordinator and catalyst for events that both educate and bring together representatives to share information and ideas.
- Small business/agency consultant specializing in strategic planning, marketing, operations and personnel.

EXPERIENCE   **Project Design and Management**

Developed and managed the Loretto Auction, the largest fund-raiser in this private school's history. (3 years)
—Recruited and managed the volunteer services of over 40 people.
—Created, built and maintained the donor base.
—Developed and refined systems for processing items.
—Marketed event to the public.
—Designed the PR materials.

Planned a national computer-use conference for over 20 Junior Leagues across the country.
—Handled logistics of catering, rooms, transportation and materials.
—Organized programs and social events.

Arranged two regional conferences for educators, a pilot program in Kansas City and another at Greenhill School in Dallas, featuring John Rassias, of Dartmouth College who is recognized nationally for his unique method of teaching foreign languages.

Served six years as Regional Chairman for the Stanford University Annual Fund, a biannual drive.
—Recruited volunteers
—Put together a phone bank

Organizational Development

Founded the Kansas City chapter of Who's Who International, a social and charitable organization for single people.

LIZ WALLY   **Page 2**

　　—Recruited members.
　　—Designed programs.
　　—Managed the budget for four years.
Created and coordinated the Independent School Group of Kansas City, a coalition of headmasters and development officers from all the city's private schools.
　　—Designed and distributed a brochure, used primarily by realtors, describing each
　　　private school.
　　—Coordinated calendars and shared strategies and information.
Built a broadly representative team to study citywide issues and produce yearly reports (adapted from the Citizen's League in Minneapolis). Once formed, the Board:
　　—Hired an executive director, research assistant and secretary.
　　—Formed three study groups (the first year).
　　—Approved and publicized the "white papers" resulting from the study groups.
　　—Evaluated, improved and continued the process.

FINANCE AND BUDGET

Served as Vice-President of the Junior League of Kansas City, with a budget of over $500,000. (2 years)
　　—Served as bookkeeper for one year, handling employee taxes, W-2 forms and
　　　insurance.
　　—Generated monthly financial reports using Peachtree General Ledger software.
　　—Chaired Finance Committee, acting as chairman of Thrift Shop (gross over
　　　$250,000).
　　—Produced new cookbook (three printings in first year).
　　—Negotiated contract dispute with printer.
　　—Reviewed projects for financial feasibility.
　　—Prepared and administered yearly budgets and audits.
　　—Worked on personnel policies, benefits and reviews.

CONSULTING

Performed consultant services for The Best of Kansas City, a firm with two retail locations and mail order business. (2 years)
　　—Interviewed and evaluated personnel.
　　—Reviewed financial and organizational systems.

EDUCATION

Stanford University, Palo Alto, California. BA 1965.

Continuing education courses in small business management and financial record keeping.

OTHER

Fluent in Spanish.
Willing to travel.

Other Good Functional Resumes

Here are some other examples of good functional resumes.

LISA BRADY
9930 Grovenor Circle
Middletown, NY 12205
518-683-9999

OBJECTIVE   A Community Relations position with the Middletown Independent School District.

PERSONAL QUALIFICATIONS

Many contacts in the corporate, academic and social service communities, cultivated over the past 15 years.

Easily establish rapport with people of all ages, cultures and philosophies.

Adept at selling ideas and programs to decision makers.

Expert in designing and presenting proposals and training programs.

Skilled in organizing events.

TEACHING EXPERIENCE

Taught kindergarten and third grade for Middletown Independent School District for 10 years.

Created and taught a pilot kindergarten program for MISD. Designed the physical environment, planned curriculum, started a parent volunteer program, budgeted and ordered supplies.

Facilitated or found speakers for over 50 training programs for administration, staff and parents of the Middletown Independent School District.

Developed a variety of volunteer programs for parents who helped with field trips, field days, classroom activities and parties.

Organized a field day for 300 people that required working with staff and volunteers, finding in-kind services, planning games, logistics and an awards ceremony.

Chaired 7 receptions honoring retirees and volunteers. Approximately 200 people attended each event.

LISA BRADY   Page 2

PUBLIC RELATIONS/SALES

Promoted and demonstrated products for Developmental Learning Materials at a national convention for educators.

Initiated and conducted over 35 information interviews with members of Middletown corporate and social service communities.

Contacted numerous members of the Middletown business and education communities in pursuit of starting an Adopt-a-School type program for MISD.

Consulted on the media campaign for Carolyn Corbin, Inc.

Served as chairman of the Public Relations committee that organized and implemented a charity softball game for the National Paralysis Association. Players included members of the Middletown Flyers and the local media. Contacted radio and television personalities about participating in media softball game.

Selected as Staff Advocate to present proposals to the MISD School Board.

Wrote public service announcements and press releases for National Paralysis Association.

Wrote monthly educational newsletter for parents and early childhood staff throughout MISD.

Served as my school's representative on the Faculty Advisory Committee, REA, and RATPE, all forums for MISD employees that develop and present ideas to the Board on topics such as career ladders, model programs and teacher evaluation.

EDUCATION

BS in Elementary Education, University of Texas at Austin, graduated with honors.

MEd in Early Childhood Education, East Texas State University, graduated with honors.

Alan McDearmon
1356 Dune Boulevard
San Diego, CA 92108
619-786-3033
619-639-2468

OBJECTIVE

Senior-level programming position that will use my extensive expertise in developing and testing complex systems.

CAREER SUMMARY

- Software professional with proven record of success in both QA and development.
- Consistently recognized by management and peers for producing high-quality work. Outstanding record for designing, coding, and thorough unit testing of software, resulting in minimal rework.
- Strong planning, communication, documentation, and support skills. Fast learner.

SYSTEMS/LANGUAGES/APPLICATIONS

UNIX	C	VAX	Apple Macintosh
Shell Scripts	COBOL	CDC NOS, NOS/VE	Microsoft Word
Assembly	Fortran	MS-DOS	Microsoft Excel

PROFESSIONAL ACHIEVEMENTS

- Software QA/Test on CDC Cyber and Mips-based CD4000 (UNIX) Series for Control Data Corporation, Santa Clara, CA
  - Conducted performance testing of Parallel Fortran on CD4000 and of C and Vector Fortran on Cyber systems. Analyzed results for conformance with design requirements. Used Excel to generate results on spreadsheets. Prompt reporting enabled developers to rapidly pinpoint areas of degradation.
  - Upgraded tools used for Fortran performance testing, allowing all testing to be completed in less than one half the previously required time. Maintained and improved the Fortran regression test tools library.
  - Enhanced Parallel Fortran performance test loader, consisting of UNIX shell scripts, to ensure consistent method of testing by all project members.
  - Developed automatic tools, including command procedures and C programs, to run regression and performance testing of the C compiler. One tool reduced processing time by two thirds by running compilation rate tests and generating final reports.
  - Wrote test plans. Developed feature, regression and performance tests noted for their thoroughness and for detecting product problems early in the test cycle.
  - Coordinated regression testing of C and Fortran. Trained other project members in testing procedures. Prepared test evaluation reports for the group.
  - Responsible for government certification of the Fortran compilers on UNIX and Cybers, which required working with the NIST validation officer. Improved all procedures and documentation, enabling other project members to assume this task with minimal assistance.

Alan McDearmon   Page 2

- Ported the complete UNIX-based Perennial C Validation Suite, which consisted of more than 250 tests, to the Cyber system.
- Revised Fortran project documentation, including instructions for setup and running of regression testing, maintenance of test and test tool libraries, problem reporting, and writing of test evaluation reports.
- Software Development and Maintenance on Cyber Series:
  - Provided the first consistent memory allocation for Cyber products by developing a Common Memory Manager. This product had the lowest number of bug reports of any member of the Cyber Product Set.
  - Designed, coded, supported and later enhanced a linking loader that resulted in significant gains in reliability, performance, maintainability and usability over the previous version.
  - Resolved more than 700 problem reports for more than 10 products.
  - Devised a tool to locate risky assembly language code sequences on Cybers using instruction stacks. This resulted in higher quality products and increased productivity for customers using these systems.
  - Enhanced the COMPASS Assembler to support new instruction sets and alternate formats for object code.
  - Improved the usability of tools for source code maintenance, project builds and project testing.
  - Designed, coded, tested and documented Task Loader for real-time transaction processing operating system (special assignment for Union Bank of Switzerland).

OTHER EXPERIENCE

Maintenance and enhancement of Cyber data management programs

Development of COBOL code generators

Development of system start-up (Deadstart) program

Software installation, including booting and configuration control

PROFESSIONAL ORGANIZATIONS

SSQA: Software Task Group of the American Society for Quality Control

EDUCATION

Software QA: Current Tools and Methodologies (UCSC Extension)

Advanced C, UNIX Shell Programming, UNIX System Calls (Control Data Corporation)

UNIX, Accelerated C Programming, Advanced C Programming, Advanced UNIX for C Programmers, Networks and Telecommunications (De Anza College, GPA 4.0)

BS Civil Engineering (Oregon State University)

George Wisdom
2100 Cameron Road
Kansas City, KS 66111
816-241-7273

POSITION OBJECTIVE
Management Consultant

BACKGROUND SUMMARY

Over 15 years' experience in all aspects of mine operation, contributing to an historic safety record. Five years of supervisory experience promoting high levels of production while building and maintaining a good safety attitude.

MAJOR ACCOMPLISHMENTS

Supervision

- In 1986 helped department to exceed production goals and deliver coal at 10% under budget. Motivated and trained employees to switch from conventional to spoil side dragline stripping.

- Supervised 24 employees, two draglines, coal loading and reclamation. Skilled at resolving day-to-day crises on the job.

- Helped to achieve the highest years of production in the history of the mine in 1985–1987. Able to build a sense of pride in the work group and create opportunities for employees to improve performance.

- Worked on special projects that included haul road construction and creek reroutes.

Heavy Equipment Operator

- Skilled at the operation and overall management of 100 cubic yard dragline. Also helped erect these draglines.

- Experienced in the operation of shovels, track dozers, haulers, scrapers and front-end loaders.

- Able to operate cable and hydraulic cranes, also rig and determine equipment limits. Knowledge of wire rope, slings and capacity charts.

- Operated and maintained over-the-road trucks for three years.

- Drove a city truck for three years.

Safety

- Assisted work unit to achieve two million manhours without a lost-time accident in 1988. Personal perfect safety record spanning 15 years.

George Wisdom
Page 2

- ∘ Conducted monthly safety meetings and trained employees in safety practices. My crew has not had a lost-time accident in over four years.
- ∘ Trained over 150 employees in handling hazardous materials.
- ∘ Capable in handling dangerous and emergency situations.
- ∘ Skilled at identifying and removing safety and health hazards.
- ∘ Certified for MSHA safety audits for surface mines, First Aid, CPR and industrial fire fighting.

EDUCATION

Baylor University—Waco, Texas	BA—Psychology
Brownfield High School—Brownfield, Texas	
Athens Training Center	Basic Mining 1983

PERSONAL

Fire Chief—Gause Volunteer Fire Department
School Board President—Gause, Independent, School District
Board of Directors—Rockdale Roping & Cutting Club
4-H Leader Milam County

"I'll have to agree with you . . . it's not exactly your run-of-the-mill resume."

7

Hybrid
Resumes

A hybrid resume combines elements of the chronological and functional formats. Separate sections often are used to describe accomplishments and work histories, but this rule isn't "poured in concrete." In fact, one of the advantages of the hybrid format is its versatility.

The Pros

Another advantage is its logical blend of the functional and chronological features. This format does the following:

☆ Concentrates on achievements rather than job titles. This is a real boon to career changers and people whose last jobs weren't their most responsible.

☆ Puts dates toward the end of the resume where gaps in employment, job-hopping and long periods at one company aren't so obvious.

☆ "Hedges your bets" if the chronological format is too rigid and the functional one too avant-garde.

Many hiring executives like this approach because it focuses on what you can do for them rather than what you have done for someone else. If a job requires several main functions, composing your resume to correspond with them delivers a uniquely explicit response to a potential employer's needs.

The Cons

Some human resources recruiters and executive search specialists are purists. They want chronological resumes. Nothing else will do. Even though job titles and dates are listed in a hybrid format, they probably won't be in the spot where these screeners expect to find them. This small break from tradition may be sufficient reason to preclude you from getting an interview.

Writing a resume that gets results is both an art and a science. Your judgment is the most critical factor when choosing between two potentially conflicting factors: how you want to present yourself versus what a potential employer expects from you. Even if your choice of format lands you in the reject pile, it's important to be true to your convictions. An employer who doesn't like your resume probably won't appreciate you either.

The examples in this chapter illustrate the variety of ways job seekers have chosen to employ this approach.

Using the Same Experience in Chronological and Hybrid Formats

John Moore, a seasoned engineer, was kind enough to send two resume examples for this book: one that search firms loved and another that helped him land interviews. Which one do you think hiring managers say they preferred because they could scan it more easily?

If you guessed that the executives prefer the hybrid resume, you're right. Isn't it interesting that people with the hiring power don't necessarily prefer the same type of format as resume screeners? This paradox becomes a real dilemma when your resume must be chosen by one group before you can advance to the next. To avoid this predicament, bypass recruiters whenever possible. This way, you can concentrate your efforts on pleasing the person who will actually become your boss.

John Moore's Hybrid Resume

JOHN B. MOORE
5641 Colgate Drive
Clinton, NY 10603
914-859-1177

OBJECTIVE   Management position involving product development, technology transfer, strategic planning, and marketing support.

SUMMARY
- Over 25 years of increasing management responsibility in various industries.
- Extensive liaison, options evaluation, project management, product development, and systems application experience.
- Planned strategies and products to meet future requirements and reduce costs.
- Supported marketing to increase market share.

EMPLOYMENT HISTORY

Worthington Industries, Inc.—Corporate Engineer	1986–present
Arvin/Diamond—Manager, Systems Engineering	1986
Bethlehem Steel Corporation—Control Systems Engineer	1972–1985

Career started in product development at ATT followed by key management roles in smaller companies.

EXPERIENCE   WORTHINGTON INDUSTRIES, INC. (Fortune 400 company with $970 million sales and 6,500 employees.)

Corporate Engineer, Product and Process Development (Reported to Vice President)

Managed program to implement the first machine vision video array systems for steel surface inspection in North America. Improved systems' performance 150%. Evaluated new technologies, equipment, vendors and product marketability. Coordinated projects, task force activities and strategic plans among nine plants and corporate home office. Managed design and development of SPC data acquisition system after surveying customers' and company's needs. Spearheaded study resulting in $3.5 million plant upgrade. Represented corporation's interests at the national level.

SUMMARY OF PREVIOUS EXPERIENCE

Management

Decreased proposal turnaround time by 25% while Systems Engineering Manager of applications group. Guided multiproduct design and development program to very successful conclusion as Engineering Department Manager of OEM product design and development group. Assumed president's duties in his absence. Turned around engineering departments' morale and improved interplant relations. Coordinated transfer of more than 30 products from laboratory development to manufacturing. Served on corporate committees.

Marketing

As Vice President for start-up company, directed all marketing and franchising activities. Researched various markets for new products to meet customers' needs. Developed and expanded companies' customer base through counselor selling. Direct advertising agency's development of marketing, sales and product literature.

Business Development/Strategic Planning

Worked with company presidents to establish corporate goals. Analyzed economic conditions, business trends and potential markets. Recommended strategies to achieve sales and profit objectives. Initiated and investigated hi-tech business opportunities. Evaluated profitability of companies' products and operations. Determined ROI for proposed equipment expenditures.

Systems/Facilities/Production

Managed development and application of more than 30 electronic control, instrumentation, and machine vision systems in small through Fortune 100 companies. Reduced systems' costs 50%. Planned hierarchical distributed and PLC control systems for 14-square-mile plant. Defined and specified the functionality of LAN and CIM systems. Handled systems' specifications, justification, quotations, procurement, vendor progress, installation, and start-up. Secured production contract by creating unique control algorithm. Planned production techniques, capital equipment expenditures and manufacturing facilities. Reduced manufacturing costs 20% by improving work flow.

EDUCATION	Princeton University, BSE in Electrical Engineering	1962
	Lehigh University, MS in Electrical Engineering	1967

PROFESSIONAL MEMBERSHIPS   SME, MVA, ISA, AISE

CIVIC ACTIVITIES   Director, Chairman, and Member of boards, authorities, and task forces.

John Moore's Chronological Resume

JOHN B. MOORE
5641 Colgate Drive
Clinton, NY 10603
914-859-1177

TECHNOLOGY DEVELOPMENT MANAGER

SUMMARY

- Experienced product and process development manager for custom products through high-volume manufacturing.
- Planned strategies to reduce costs, improve quality, and meet future requirements.
- Extensive liaison, task definition, options evaluation, project management, and systems application experience.
- Supported marketing to increase market share.
- 25 years of increasing management responsibility in various industries.

EXPERIENCE

1986–1994   **WORTHINGTON INDUSTRIES, INC.** (Holding company for manufacturing companies in multiple industries and markets)

Corporate Engineer, Product and Process Development (Reported to Vice President)

Initiated and investigated hi-tech business opportunities. Worldwide evaluations of new technologies, equipment and vendors. Coordinated projects, task force activities and strategic plans among plants and home office. Managed program to implement the first machine vision video array systems for steel surface inspection in North America (improved systems' performance 150%). Managed design and development of SPC data acquisition system after surveying customers' and company's needs. Evaluated profitability of subsidiary's products and operations; then spearheaded study resulting in $3.5 million plant upgrade. Investigated acoustic emission, microencapsulation, electrostatic painting and factory automation technologies. Represented corporation at the national level.

1986   **DIAMOND ELECTRONICS, INC.** (Division of Arvin Industries until sold in June, 1986)

Manager, Systems Engineering (Reported to Vice President)

Managed applications group responsible for engineering custom, computer-based distributed access control and industrial CCTV systems. Decreased proposal turnaround time by 25%. Developed and expanded company's customer base through supporting Sales' efforts. Served on product line review committee.

1972–1985   **BETHLEHEM STEEL COMPANY**

Control Systems Engineer   (1981–1985 at Bethlehem Plant)

Project team leader for over 10 in-house and turnkey machinery and real-time control systems. Defined systems' functions, design criteria and cost

JOHN B. MOORE   **Page 2**

justification analyses for proposed equipment with users and vendors. Evaluated computers and PLCs as options for control systems. Strategic planning of plantwide, hierarchical, distributed control and LAN systems for 14-square-mile plant. Served on corporate LAN and computer committees.

Electrical Engineer   (1977–1981 at Bethlehem Plant)
(Promoted to Control Systems Engineer)
Designed, modernized, and installed instrumentation, controls and computers. Handled systems' procurement and supervised vendors. Hands-on assistance of craftsmen during start-up, troubleshooting and repair. Served on corporate computer maintenance committee.

Research Engineer   (1972–1977 at Homer Research Laboratories)
(Promoted to Electrical Engineer)
Developed nondestructive testing systems for corporatewide steel operations.

1970–1972   **GALT CONTROLS, INC.**
Engineering Manager (Reported to President)
Managed design and development of electronic assemblies for OEM controls for commercial, consumer and medical products. Guided multiproduct manufacturing development efforts to very successful conclusions. Responsible for product specifications, designs, quotations, and production techniques. Corrected department's morale problem. Analyzed economic conditions, business trends and potential markets. Worked with president to establish corporate goals and assumed his duties in his absence. Close liaison with customers to define, determine feasibility and develop new products.

1969–1970   **SURCOM SYSTEMS, INC.**
Vice President of Marketing (Reported to President)
Directed all marketing and training activities for a new company making security systems.

1968–1969   **ALL AMERICAN ENGINEERING COMPANY**
Project Engineer
Proposed and designed commercial and military controls. Reduced design times by reassigning designers' duties (also improved group's morale).

1962–1968   **WESTERN ELECTRIC COMPANY** (Includes one year in Bell Telephone Laboratories)
Development Engineer
Coordinated transfer of more than 30 semiconductors from laboratory to manufacturing. Reduced testing and reliability costs 20% by improving work flow on product development lines. Planned production techniques, equipment requirements and budgets.

EDUCATION   Princeton University, BSE in Electrical Engineering   1962
Lehigh University, MS in Electrical Engineering   1967

PROFESSIONAL MEMBERSHIPS   SME, MVA, ISA, AISE

CIVIC ACTIVITIES   Director, Chairman, and Member on boards, authorities and task forces.

Two Objectives, Two Resumes, Same Experience

After a brief stint in retail management, Mark Slagle worked for five years in his family's country club business. While he enjoyed supervising clubhouse activities, he decided his long-term opportunities were better outside the family firm. To make the move he targeted both property and club management, and prepared somewhat different resumes to highlight his background for each type of position.

Country or City Club Management

MARK SLAGLE
373 Copeland Drive
Addison, TX 75248
214-779-2650

OBJECTIVE   Club management position with Club Corporation International, where I can use my experience in selling memberships and catering.

EMPLOYMENT HISTORY

1988–present   Clubhouse Manager, Twin Timbers Country Club, Dallas, Texas.

Working with Public

- Sold memberships by showing prospective members the facilities and explaining the amenities at Twin Timbers Country Club.
- Planned functions for both members and nonmembers such as wedding receptions, Christmas parties, and golf outings attended by 50–1,000 people.
- Negotiated contractual arrangements for the above activities.
- Handled member complaints with speed and diplomacy.

Administration

- Purchased over $100,000 of supplies for clubhouse each year.
- Supervised a staff of 5–10 people.
- Held general management responsibility for a 650-member club including food and beverage, monthly newsletter, accounting, payroll and membership.

Maintenance

- Scheduled and delegated daily maintenance for a 40,000-square-foot club house and its surrounding grounds.
- Assured that two commercial kitchens met health department standards.
- Contracted with 20 vendors who provided service for electricity, plumbing, pest control, air conditioning, etc.

1985–1988   Manager & Sales for Curtis Mathis Store, Dallas, Texas.

- Finished in top 5 salespeople for Dallas/Ft. Worth each month.
- Sold an average of $15,000 per month in home entertainment products.
- Youngest Store Manager in area.

EDUCATION   BA Economics, Southern Methodist University, graduated cum laude

Property Management

MARK SLAGLE
373 Copeland Drive
Addison, TX 75248
214-779-2650

OBJECTIVE   Property management position with Carter-Crawley where I can use my experience in dealing with people and managing a large facility.

QUALIFICATIONS AND EXPERIENCE

WORKING WITH TENANTS

- Sold memberships by showing prospective members the facilities and explaining the amenities at Twin Timbers Country Club.
- Planned functions for both members and nonmembers such as wedding receptions, Christmas parties, and golf outings attended by 50–1,000 people.
- Negotiated contractual arrangements for the above activities.
- Handled member complaints with speed and diplomacy.

OFFICE ADMINISTRATION

- Purchased over $100,000 of supplies for clubhouse each year.
- Supervised a staff of 5–10 people.
- Held general management responsibility for a 650-member club including food and beverage, monthly newsletter, accounting, pay roll and membership.

PROPERTY MAINTENANCE

- Scheduled and delegated daily maintenance for a 40,000-square-foot clubhouse and its surrounding grounds.
- Assured that two commercial kitchens met health department standards.
- Contracted with 20 vendors who provided service for electricity, plumbing, pest control, air conditioning, etc.

EMPLOYMENT EXPERIENCE

1988–present	Clubhouse Manager, Twin Timbers Country Club, Dallas, Texas.
1985–1988	Manager & Sales for Curtis Mathis Store, Dallas, Texas.

EDUCATION   BA Economics, Southern Methodist University, graduated cum laude

Matching Functions to Objectives

Mike Benton had a successful career in insurance and banking, but wasn't particularly satisfied. In working with a career counselor, he decided he would like a profession that was more people oriented. He chose several that he thought would provide opportunities close to his ideal job description. They were personal financial planning, trust management, fund raising, nonprofit management, training and development, and public speaking. To prepare resumes for each of these careers, he put together an accomplishments history, then distilled it into a group of six functional experience areas as follows:

COMMUNITY INVOLVEMENT

• Served on Board of Urban Services YMCA and as Division Leader of Annual Campaign, 1990.

• Active on Board of the Way Back House and on fund-raising committee.

• Participated as Administrative Board Member and teacher, Highland Park Methodist Church.

• Contributed many hours as coach and leader for YMCA Youth Sports and Indian Guides.

• Active Dallas native with numerous contacts developed in civic, business and educational sectors.

BUSINESS DEVELOPMENT

• Developed and managed $13 million loan portfolio for 175 customers composed of corporate executives, doctors, attorneys, CPAs, wealthy individuals and private companies.

• Built a $3 million life insurance practice in 1½ years serving 100 upper-income clients.

• Recruited, trained, and developed a unit of five life insurance agents producing over $5 million in insurance sales in a 12-month period.

• Planned and implemented new business development program for S&L branch; awarded President's Trophy for top production.

LEADERSHIP AND MANAGEMENT

• Developed and staffed the management training department as a new function; administered departmental budget.

• Managed $10 million S&L office including loan production, operations and staffing.

• Commanded an artillery battery of 100 men and led the battalion with recognition as Best Battery-Army Commendation Medal.

• Led the Texas Aggie Band as Head Drum Major-Distinguished Military Graduate.

CONSULTING

• Advised Southwestern Life senior executives regarding training and development needs and solutions for field managers.

• Provided financial counseling for insurance clients in areas of budgeting, wills, trusts, insurance and educational planning.

• Consulted with corporate bank customers on cash flow, liquidity, expansion, asset planning and tax issues related to credit loans.

FINANCIAL PLANNING AND ANALYSIS

• Performed evaluations of corporate and personal financial statements using ratios, trends, cash flow projections and liquidity analysis.

• Implemented and supervised use of Coopers & Lybrand system for estate planning.

TRAINING AND DEVELOPMENT

• Planned, created and implemented the Southwestern Life Agency Management Training Program for company use in 35 branch offices.

• Organized, designed and conducted 10 company training schools for managers. Also served as primary instructor.

• Certified leader/trainer for Counselor Selling, Wilson Learning.

• Coordinated and taught 12 branch schools in both basic and advanced subjects including estate planning and pensions.

• Conducted monthly staff development meetings for bank loan officers.

When tailoring his resume for specific job openings, Mike selected functional areas that parallel his objective. Included here are two resumes that Mike customized for positions in financial planning and fund raising. Notice how they are similar yet distinct. If you are changing careers and pursuing several fields, you might want to try this approach. It allows you to prepared tailored versions of your resume without having to start each one from scratch.

Mike's job search led to a position in trust banking, which he held for several years. Mike has since decided to become a financial planner now that his children are older, his wife has returned to teaching and the family has a financial cushion.

Financial Planning Resume

Michael B. Benton
6591 Utica Road
Dallas, TX 75222

H: 214-231-7570
W: 214-437-8967

OBJECTIVE

Consultative Financial Planning position that requires relationship building skills and a proven business development background.

PERSONAL QUALIFICATIONS

- Adept at establishing trust and credibility with the public.
- Strong communication skills, with 18 years in business and civic activities, as an instructor, business trainer, coach and public speaker.
- Consistent record of managing projects and details to get results.
- Mission/achievement motivated with a concern for helping others.
- A quick learner who enjoys keeping current with new developments in my field and at large.

EXPERIENCE AND SKILLS

Business Development

- Developed and managed $13 million loan portfolio for 175 customers composed of corporate executives, doctors, attorneys, CPAs, wealthy individuals and private companies.
- Built a $3 million life insurance practice in $1\frac{1}{2}$ years serving 100 upper-income clients.
- Recruited, trained, and developed a unit of five life insurance agents producing over $5 million in insurance sales in a 12-month period.
- Planned and implemented new business development program for S&L branch; awarded President's Trophy for top production.

Consulting

- Advised Southwestern Life senior executives regarding training and development needs and solutions for field managers.
- Provided financial counseling for insurance clients in areas of budgeting, wills, trusts, insurance and educational planning.
- Consulted with corporate bank customers on cash flow, liquidity, expansion, asset planning and tax issues related to credit loans.

Financial Planning and Analysis

- Performed evaluations of corporate and personal financial statements using ratios, trends, cash flow projections and liquidity analysis.
- Implemented and supervised use of Coopers & Lybrand system for estate planning.

EMPLOYMENT HISTORY
Commercial Banking
- Vice President, Commercial Lending, Cullen Frost Bank, 1985 to present
- Vice President, Manager, Professional and Executive Lending, Interfirst Bank, 1982-1985

Insurance
- Southwestern Life Insurance Company, 1976-1982, Sales Manager, Director of Corporate Management Training, Life Insurance Agent

Mortgage Banking
- First Texas Savings, 1972-1976, Branch Manager, Assistant Manager, Loan Officer

EDUCATION
- BBA—Finance/Marketing, Texas A&M University, Distinguished Student
- Graduate Studies, Southern Methodist University
- 250 hours in Professional Development courses and Continuing Education
- CLU Candidate, The American College
- Dale Carnegie course, graduate and former instructor
- Toastmasters Club, 3 years

Development Resume

Michael B. Benton   H: 214-231-7570
6591 Utica Road   W: 214-437-8967
Dallas, TX 75222

OBJECTIVE: Development position that requires relationship-building skills and a proven business development background

PERSONAL QUALIFICATIONS
- Adept at establishing trust and credibility with the public.
- Strong communication skills, with 18 years in business and civic activities, as an instructor, business trainer, coach, and public speaker.
- Consistent record of managing projects and details to get results.
- Mission/achievement motivated with a concern for helping others.
- A quick learner who enjoys keeping current with new developments in my field and at large.

EXPERIENCE AND SKILLS
BUSINESS DEVELOPMENT

- Developed and managed $13 million loan portfolio for 175 customers composed of corporate executives, doctors, attorneys, CPAs, wealthy individuals, and private companies.
- Built a $3 million life insurance practice in $1\frac{1}{2}$ years serving 100 upper-income clients.
- Recruited, trained, and developed a unit of five life insurance agents producing over $5 million in insurance sales in a 12-month period.
- Planned and implemented new business development program for S&L branch; awarded President's Trophy for top production.

COMMUNITY INVOLVEMENT

- Served on Board of Urban Services YMCA and as Division Leader of Annual Campaign, 1990.
- Active on Board of the Way Back House and on fund-raising committee.
- Participated as Administrative Board Member and teacher, Highland Park Methodist Church.
- Contributed many hours as coach and leader for YMCA Youth Sports and Indian Guides.
- Active Dallas native with numerous contacts developed in civic, business, and educational sectors.

Michael B. Benton   Page 2

LEADERSHIP AND MANAGEMENT

- Provided financial counseling for insurance clients in areas of budgeting, wills, trusts, insurance and educational planning.
- Implemented and supervised use of Coopers & Lybrand system for estate planning.
- Consulted with corporate bank customers on cash flow, liquidity, expansion, asset planning and tax issues related to credit lines.
- Performed evaluations of corporate and personal financial statements using ratios, trends, cash flow projections and liquidity analysis.

EMPLOYMENT HISTORY

COMMERCIAL BANKING

- Vice President, Commercial Lending, Cullen Frost Bank, 1985 to present
- Vice President, Manager, Professional and Executive Lending, Interfirst Bank, 1982-1985

INSURANCE

- Southwestern Life Insurance Company, 1976-1982, Sales Manager, Director of Corporate Management Training, Life Insurance Agent

MORTGAGE BANKING

- First Texas Savings, 1972-1976, Branch Manager, Assistant Manager, Loan Officer

EDUCATION

- BBA—Finance/Marketing, Texas A&M University, Distinguished Student
- Graduate Studies, Southern Methodist University
- 250 hours in Professional Development courses and Continuing Education
- CLU Candidate, The American College
- Dale Carnegie course, graduate and former instructor
- Toastmasters Club, 3 years

Other Good Hybrid Resumes

Candidates in a variety of careers prepared the collection of hybrid resumes that follow.

ARDELLA Y. MILES
5535 Vermont Drive
Burlington, CT 06470
Home: 203-994-4833
Work: 203-994-9807

OBJECTIVE   A management position with a focus on the administration of client relations, marketing management, and systems implementation.

SUMMARY OF QUALIFICATIONS

- 12 years of experience in Global Cash Management and Auditing
- 6 years of successful product and technical marketing administered to Fortune 1000 Companies and Financial Institutions
- Strength in the evaluation and analysis of operational work flows
- Skills in product research and strategic planning analysis

EMPLOYMENT
HISTORY   Mellon Bank, NA, Philadelphia, PA

1986–Present   Product Manager
                  Collections & Disbursement Services
                  Remittance Processing Services

1980–1986   Audit Supervisor

RELEVANT SKILLS AND ACCOMPLISHMENTS

Client Relations and Marketing Management: Developed valuable professional rapport with operations managers, marketing officers, and clients and set standards for product development, service delivery, and customer relations. Collaborated with marketing representatives on sales calls and provided the technical support to close deals. Successfully implemented 15 new disbursement relationships and increased the $6 million revenue base during 1991. Developed and instructed cash management product seminars.

Quality Assurance: Successfully led a team of diversified managers to improve the operating performance in the delivery of the collections and disbursement services during 1991 and 1992. Coordinated the efforts to ensure the implementation and achievement of quality standards for total customer satisfaction.

Project Management: Planned, prioritized and assigned projects administered by the Product Management team. Projects focused on the integration of operation systems to improve the process and delivery of services. Developed business and strategic plans between 1988 and 1991 and increased the volume and revenue generated from the Philadelphia client base.

EDUCATION	BS, Finance and Marketing, GPA 3.1 Clarion University—Pennsylvania, 1979
AWARDS AND RECOGNITION	Mellon PSFS Chairman's Award for Sales and Service Excellence—JUNE 1992 Premier Achievement Awards—1989 and 1992 Client Support Recognition from Chase Manhattan Bank (USA)
PROFESSIONAL AFFILIATIONS	Financial Women International Pennsylvania Commission for Women

CLAUDIA DIXON

9127 Hill Place   214-387-3245
Irving, TX 75060   214-938-6276

OBJECTIVE   Assistant Director at Dispute Mediation Service of Dallas, Inc.

QUALIFICATIONS
- BA Rice University, Houston, Texas, Phi Beta Kappa.
- Mediator Certification through DMS, 40 hours, May 1990.
- Additional 24 CEUs, East Texas State University, October 1990, Family Dynamics, Child Development, and Family Law.
- Seven years' experience in word processing and data entry.
- Fourteen years' office experience in profit and nonprofit settings.

SKILLS

Administration/Organization
- Process information accurately and organize data logically.
- Plan and organize work efficiently, good follow-through with careful attention to detail.
- Manage office-coordinating responsibilities to meet needs of all parties, ensuring smooth functioning of up to four businesses.
- Handle many duties concurrently—bookkeeping, telephone work, word processing, editing material for publication, requisition of office supplies, accounts payable and receivable, scheduling and client contact.

Oral and Written Communication
- Mediate and co-mediate a variety of disputes for DMS.
- Effectively promote and explain services of diverse businesses both in person and using excellent telephone skills.
- Create clear, concise correspondence, brochures, newsletters, reports and training materials.
- Instruct groups of up to 40 adults and adolescents in public school, social service agency and community college settings.

EMPLOYMENT HISTORY

Office Manager,   Dimensions Associates, 1984 to present
                    Genie Weitzman, 1980–84
                    The Heart Center, 1978–80

Associate Director, Employment Information Service, Women's Center of Dallas, 1977–78. Employed in this capacity after working as a volunteer in the Employment Information Service.

Teacher, Austin Independent School District, 1967–69

WILLIAM C. KEYES
Davenport Apartments
1765 Caulfield Road
Philadelphia, PA 19140
(215) 565-8988 (OFFICE) (215) 342-8499 (HOME)

OBJECTIVE

Position as a manager for Affirmative Action where developing relationships with the minority community is a prerequisite.

AREAS OF EXPERTISE

Accomplishments

- While employed with the Wharton West Philadelphia Project, increased recruitment effort from 12 entrepreneur companies to 42 entrepreneur companies.
- Placed over 3,000 youths with the PHIL-A-JOB Program.
- Fund Raising and Proposal writing effort generated over $5 million.
- Serviced the Philadelphia community over a period of 20 years, by creating better ways of delivering employment and services.

Project Management

- Served in Human Resources capacity, as well as Affirmative Action Specialist with Philadelphia Urban Affairs Coalition and Philadelphia Urban League.
- Coordinated first citywide program for minority employment in private sector. Supervised staff of 31, delivered 3,000 placements among 400 major corporations.
- Conceived, planned and implemented neighborhood revitalization project involving 400 single-family units.
- Supervised 30 employees in administration and funding of children's day care facility in conjunction with major pediatric medical center.
- Implement the first Economic Development Project, Shopping Center Strip for the Wharton West Philadelphia Project.

Business Development

- Provided full range of start-up support services: Business plan, solicitation of financial backing and marketing. Assisted in the funding of 300 entrepreneurs.
- Management consultant delivering quality marketing, sales and related advisory services to entrepreneurs.
- Developed expertise in qualifying private business for certification with the city of Philadelphia, Minority Business Enterprise (MBE) and Women Business Enterprise (WBE). Prepare successful proposals for city, state and federal contracts for WBE and MBE businesses.

William C. Keyes   **Page 2**

Public Relations

- Designed and developed advertising campaigns for entrepreneurs, wrote press releases and coordinated special events.
- Acted as spokesman for agency. Attended company affairs and delivered speeches.

Financial

- Directed broad-based financial aid services for student groups of approximately 1,500. Initiated alternative funding as needed.
- Negotiated funding in excess of $5 million. Administered monies in broad range of social programs, assisted in audits and final reports.
- Major fund-raising activities, ranging from $20,000 to $5 million.

EMPLOYMENT HISTORY

WHARTON WEST PHILADELPHIA PROJECT	1-14-91 to PRESENT
Wharton School, University of Pennsylvania	Assistant Director
PHILADELPHIA URBAN AFFAIRS COALITION	1980–1990
Human Resources Manager	
Business Development Consultant	
Philadelphia Business Academy (ON LOAN FROM PUAC)	1979–1980
Placement Manager/Trainer	
TEMPLE UNIVERSITY	1977–1979
Project Manager of Financial Aid	
PHILADELPHIA COUNCIL FOR COMMUNITY ADVANCEMENT	1976–1977
Housing Manager	
REBOUND DAY CARE CENTER	1974–1976
Administrator	

EDUCATION

UNIVERSITY OF PENNSYLVANIA, Candidate for MBA	1969–1972
Wharton School, Management/Industrial Relations	
CHEYNEY STATE UNIVERSITY, Education/Teaching, Bachelor of Science	1965–1967
FELS CENTER OF GOVERNMENT, University of Pennsylvania	1972
THE URBAN LEAGUE LEADERSHIP INSTITUTE	1991

GERALD C. JACOBSON
34779 Haviland Drive
Detroit, MI 48236
313-677-6634

SUMMARY

Senior executive with extensive experience in all aspects of financial management in mid-size to large corporations. Possesses strong managerial, communications and organizational skills.

ACCOMPLISHMENTS

Financial

- Directed financial programs and coordinated the efforts of investment bankers, outside counsel and state officials to construct three facilities with tax-exempt public financing.
- Developed, in conjunction with operating management, business plans to be used by the Board of Directors to evaluate projects and the financial community to make lending decisions.
- Instituted an automated cash concentration system resulting in quicker availability and the ability to manage and more effectively use excess funds.
- Maintained relationships with both commercial banks and investment banking institutions. Negotiated terms, waivers and amendments to loan agreements.
- Directed design and implementation of computerized and standardized accounting systems, resulting in improved reporting of financial results and the ability to analyze variances from plan.
- Resolved a $5,500,000 insurance claim and directed the corporate risk-management program.

Accounting and Control

- Managed information systems, treasury, financial analysis, forecasting, budgeting, planning, tax and credit functions with over 60 staff members. Improved systems and organized workload, both to keep staffing under control during periods of growth and to still "get the job done" during periods of downsizing.
- Integrated accounting functions for a number of business units resulting in the elimination of duplicate overhead and improved control over operations.
- Provided necessary reports on a timely basis to the Securities and Exchange Commission including 10Qs and 10Ks.
- Directed efforts of outside auditors resulting in timely completion and control over audit fees.

Taxes

- Organized tax planning efforts to take advantage of opportunities to minimize tax liability.
- Negotiated a tax abatement for a $26,000,000 capital improvement program.
- Managed all federal and local tax reporting in a multicompany environment, avoiding late filing and other noncompliance penalties.

PROFESSIONAL EXPERIENCE

Envotech Management Services, Inc.

Treasurer/CFO	1989–Present
Controller	1988–1989

McLouth Steel Products Corporation

Controller/Assistant Treasurer	1984–1988
Controller	1984

White Motor Corporation

Controller	1981–1984
Assistant Controller	1979–1981
Director, Corporate Financial Accounting	1977–1979

Ernst & Young

Audit Manager	1972–1977
Audit Supervisor	1969–1972
Accountant	1964–1969

EDUCATION

BBA Cleveland State University
Certified Public Accountant—Ohio

PROFESSIONAL ORGANIZATIONS

Financial Executive Institute	Ohio Society of CPAs
American Institute of CPAs	Trenton Athletic Club

"You stated on your application that you have a bizarre sense of humor . . . could you be more specific?"

8

Resumes for Consulting, Freelancing, Volunteer and Internal Company Use

G enerally when people think about writing a resume, they expect to send it to a future employer. That's a common use, but certainly not the only one. Professionals also need resumes to:

- ☆ Include in consulting proposals.
- ☆ Secure freelance contracts.
- ☆ Apply for positions within their own firm.

☆   Provide when requested for Board of Director or key committee positions in profit or nonprofit organizations.

Resumes for these purposes follow no hard-and-fast rules, but nonetheless have some similarities. All concentrate on accomplishments specifically tailored to the resume recipient's requirements. Many mention names of clients, task forces and projects that their readers will recognize. Job titles and dates aren't particularly significant because the length or date of a consulting or freelance assignment has little to do with its success, and an employee's contribution to her company is more important than her longevity.

Internal Resumes

These resumes are prepared by professionals who seek to advance within their companies. Typically, they illustrate the significance of their work and their eligibility for higher-level positions. Notice that the formats for the examples of internal resumes that follow are quite different yet equally effective.

Ann Fiorelli

After buying MTech, EDS Corporation installed its own management within the acquired company. As a former EDS employee, Ann's new boss was unfamiliar with her work at MTech. He asked her for a short summary of her projects to give him a better feel for her background. Ann provided the resume that follows.

Ann has since moved to the Dallas office of Andersen Consulting where she is a manager in business development for one of its four major business service lines.

ANN L. FIORELLI
1040 Trailen Road
Irving, TX 75063
Home: 214-366-5305
Work: 214-715-8858

OBJECTIVE

To develop marketing and communications programs for a service-driven organization.

SKILLS

Creating conceptualizing, communicating, consulting, selling, managing, training, coordinating, planning and promoting.

ACCOMPLISHMENTS

Created a marketing information department for a high-tech service organization. Helped the company grow from $63 million to $235 million in annual revenue by identifying emerging trends and needs within the financial services industry.

Contributed to the production of more than $1 million in new revenue, promoted client retention and enhanced the company's image using communications tools including presentations, seminars, trade shows, television, brochures, newsletters, advertising, proposals, reports, speeches, interviews, special events, direct mail and telemarketing.

Consulted with clients about developing products, targeting markets and selling the benefits of their products and services.

Designed and implemented a fund-raising campaign for the Easter Seal Society. Generated the highest participation rate, 16%, of all corporate fund-raisers and brought in the greatest number of first-time contributors.

Designed a marketing database to increase net profits by $94,000 in one year by targeting markets and identifying cross-sales opportunities.

Selected and worked with vendors including designers, printers, sign companies, manufacturers and research suppliers.

Staffed and managed a 20–30 person department that recruited participants for marketing research studies. Cut costs by $1/3$ in less than six months.

Designed and facilitated pilot programs to evaluate marketability of new products and services. Trained customers and colleagues to implement procedures, solicited corporate sponsorships and developed promotional strategies based on results.

Ann L. Fiorelli   **Page 2**

ASSOCIATIONS

American Marketing Association: Work with the board to develop programs, increase membership and enhance the benefits of belonging to the association.

Dallas Easter Seal Society: Consult with fund-raisers for the upcoming corporate campaign.

Texas Computer Industry Council: Developed business case and plan for profiling high-tech companies in Texas.

Dallas Committee for Foreign Visitors: Plan activities and give tours of the city to visitors on business from other countries.

Irving Men's Baseball Association: Solicited publicity for the association that resulted in league expansion.

EMPLOYERS

EDS/MTech: August 1982 to present.

Southwest Research, Inc.: January 1979 to June 1982.

EDUCATION

BA Communications—"Honors Graduate"—The University of New Mexico.

Martin Mueller

Martin was an industrial truck driver (hauler) at a surface mining operation in East Texas. An ambitious young man, he decided the best way to advance his career was to earn a college degree, so he enrolled full time at the University of Texas at Tyler. Since he had a family to support, he arranged to work the graveyard shift—7 P.M. to 7 A.M. After work, he drove 60 miles to attend classes until 1 or 2 P.M. He typically slept only three or four hours before returning to work, and studied while his hauler was being loaded with coal.

Martin graduated magna cum laude in four years, earning a 3.8 GPA in Industrial Technology and Speech Communication. He structured his resume to highlight this amazing feat. Within a year of graduation, he was promoted to the position of Industrial Technician.

Martin Mueller
Springfield North
Work: 413-683-5408
Home: 413-954-6583

SUMMARY

Over 19 years' experience in heavy industrial settings, including equipment operation (trucking) and machine tool production runs. Recently graduated magna cum laude from University of Texas at Tyler with majors in Industrial Technology and Speech Communication. Excellent at maintaining high-quality work and communicating information clearly and accurately. Dedicated to achieving personal and organizational goals.

ACADEMIC HISTORY

Bachelor of Science Degree from University of Texas at Tyler conferred magna cum laude. 3.8/4.0 GPA. Degree was earned while working a full-time 12-hour rotating shift and carrying 15 semester hours. A 150-mile round-trip commute was required daily.

Academic honors include:
President's Honor Society
Dean's List
Alpha Chi National Honor and Scholarship Society
Who's Who Among Students in American Universities and Colleges

WORK EXPERIENCE

Industrial Operations
Eight years' experience in operating 100-ton hauler safely and under a variety of weather conditions. Perfect safety record. Able to monitor equipment status and report operational problems.

Owner/Operator of Trucking Business
Scheduled and supervised loading, transporting, and unloading of various materials. Scheduled and performed all maintenance, service and repairs on equipment.

Machinist
Performed all phases of production runs from setup through inspection. Machine tool experience includes numerical control, mills, lathes, grinders, planer, profile, and drills in aviation, electronic and oil field applications. Commonly held tolerances were plus or minus .001 inch. Tolerances as close as .0003 inch were maintained in some production runs. Adept at working very carefully, being exact and accurate in completing each task.

Martin Mueller   **Page 2**

Sales/Public Relations
Developed and expanded prospect list for property sales. Conducted cold calls to
provide prospects with information concerning property. Supervised a crew of men
in the operation, maintenance, and upkeep of property. Skilled at public speaking
and adult education. Currently using these skills in voluntary situations.

WORK HISTORY

Texas Utilities Mining Company	Hauler Operator	1982–Present
Owner/Operator Trucking Business		1979–1982
Container Machinery Incorporated	Machinist	1978–1979

OTHER HIGHLIGHTS

Hobbies: Reading, Golf, Travel

Consultant Resumes

Here are some examples of the types of resume consultants use when submitting client proposals to secure contracts on a project or retainer basis.

Henri Vezina

Henri, a human resources consultant since 1986, includes this resume in client information packages and proposals. Notice how he highlights the corporations that have used his services and the projects he has completed for them. In his case, "name-dropping" is more important than quantified accomplishments because potential clients will assume that if he was hired by Digital, Kodak and DuPont, he must know what he's doing.

HENRI A. VEZINA
4 North Prince Street
Belle Grove, NH 03049
603-783-1495

EXPERIENCE
1986–Pres.   Human Resources Management Consultant
- Provide strong expertise in all areas of Human Resources; management consulting, employment, employee relations, compensation, AA/EEO, information systems and training.

Clients:
- **Datasec Corporation**, Wilton, NH
  Management consulting, employee relations, compensation, employment, training, administration

- **Digital Equipment Corporation**, Hudson, Littleton, Marlboro, MA
  Counseling, employment, training, info system, outplacement

- **Du Pont Imagitex**, Nashua, NH
  Employment, employee relations, policies and procedures, ADA

- **Kodak's Electronic Printing Systems Group**, Bedford, MA
  Vice-President's advisor, evaluation of R&D managers

- **Morton International**, Seabrook, NH
  Staff advisor, employee relations, union avoidance

- **Stratus Computer, Inc.**, Marlboro, MA
  Employment, employee relations, info system, training

- **VMark Software, Inc.**, Natick, MA
  Policies & Procedures manual, AA/EEO plan, compensation program

- **White Pine Software, Inc.**, Amherst, NH
  Management consulting, Policies & Procedures, training.

1985–1986   **CHORUS DATA SYSTEMS, INC.**, Merrimack, NH
CUNEIFORM SYSTEMS, INC., Nashua, NH
Human Resources Director for parent company and subsidiary.

- Reported to the Chairman of the Board; advised and supported the Presidents of both companies and their staffs.

- Responsible for establishing the Personnel functions for both companies; policy and procedure administration, recruitment, employee relations, compensation and benefits.

- When both companies closed, counseled 90+ employees and coordinated outplacement of individuals into other companies.

Henri A. Vezina   Page 2

1983–1985   APOLLO COMPUTER, INC., Chelmsford, MA
                Human Resources Manager for Engineering Organization

- Advisor to five Engineering Vice-Presidents
- Hired and managed staff of five who provided all Personnel services—employee relations, compensation, employment and management/employee development.
- Developed and directed Apollo's recruitment program.
- Established company's computerized applicant tracking system.

1974–1983   DIGITAL EQUIPMENT CORPORATION
                Progressed from entry level Personnel Representative to Human Resources Supervisor (5 levels)

                Commercial Engineering, Merrimack, NH, '80 to '83
                Computer Special Systems, Nashua, NH, '77 to '80
                Central Engineering and Manufacturing, Maynard, MA, '74 to '77

- Hired, trained and managed staff at each of the sites.
- Provided employee relations, compensation, career counseling, and training to management and employees.
- Designed automated employment tracking system that was adopted by other DEC Employment groups.
- Managed complete recruiting function for all groups.
- Strong leadership role in Corporate Compensation's effort to rewrite Engineering and Manufacturing job descriptions.
- Conducted compensation survey of local area hi-tech companies.

EDUCATION
- Extensive course work in Management at University of New Hampshire, Boston University, and National Training Labs.
- Conducted Personnel Courses and Seminars at New Hampshire Colleges

SYSTEMS
- DEC, IMB PC, Stratus, Apollo Workstations

NOTE
- Speak, read and write French.

Kathy Halbrooks

Kathy was one of the many managers laid off from SEI Corp. during a restructuring. Because she enjoyed working with clients in the employee benefits arena, she decided to stay in that field. After interviewing with several large benefits administration firms, she resolved to start her own company.

Today Kathy owns K. Halbrooks and Associates and American Voice Link. K. Halbrooks and Associates is an employee benefits administration firm that served 120 businesses after only 18 months in operation. American Voice Link is just getting off the ground with an initial customer base of about 90 voice mailboxes.

Kathy Halbrooks
2930 Rowland Court
Prestonwood, TN 37203
615-794-1390

Objective

Employee Benefits Consultant with a national firm recognized for its expertise in qualified employee benefit plans.

Professional Highlights

- Eleven years of progressively responsible experience in employee benefit plans in both in-house plan management and third-party consulting and management.
- Build rapport and trust quickly with clients and colleagues.
- Particularly enjoy developing employee communications campaigns using video presentations, employee information packets and human resources training programs.
- Handle many projects simultaneously with minimal stress.

Experience

SEI Corporation, 1988–1993

Director of Plan Services

- Managed approximately 80 client plans, which provide benefits for more than 100,000 participants.
- Served as the final authority in resolving client issues.
- Developd and implement training programs to educate and update employees on regulations governing qualified plans.
- Supervised a staff of 35 people who are responsible for the day-to-day administrative functions of our client programs.
- Personally provided marketing support services for all West Coast sales.

Director of Professional Services

- Consulted both internally and with SEI clients on plan testing, qualification requirements and analysis of projections to determine participation levels.
- Coordinated employee communications program for Toyota Motor Sales, USA. Worked with a production company to develop a 10-minute videotape to introduce SEI and its services, and educate

Kathy Halbrooks   **Page 2**

employees on investing. Put together a slide presentation to further explain the plan enhancements. Designed an employee information packet. Trained human resources staff on how to present the materials to employees. Campaign served as a prototype for other SEI clients.

- Developed a prototype plan for SEI to be used both as a mass submitter as well as sponsoring organization.
- Used extensive network of contacts in the employee benefits industry to build a highly effective, experienced staff.

Employee Benefits Consultant, 1987–1988

- Assisted human resources management at MTech and SEI in evaluating policies and procedures, and making improvements as necessary.

Actuarial Assistant, Diversified Consultants, 1985–1987

- Coordinated the day-to-day administration of several qualified plans. Responsibilities ranged from actuarial valuations to preparation of government filings.

Senior Account Representative, JTV&A, 1981–1985

- Administered operation of defined benefits and defined contribution plans for 85 clients.

Education

BA in Advertising, The University of Texas
S.E.C. Registration Series 6
Completed ASPA courses 1 and 2

Organizations

Member, Tennessee Pension Society
Member, Southwest Pension Association
Member, National Association of Female Executives

Interests

Running, biking, swimming and participating in triathlons.

Patricia Gifford

Pat is a psychotherapist with a number of years' experience in a variety of therapeutic settings. Because many employers are offering medical insurance under the umbrella of preferred provider groups, Pat often needs to send her resume to coordinators who select providers for their networks. The following resume contains the background information she forwards to each of the provider groups who might be interested in her services.

PATRICIA A. GIFFORD, CSW ACP
43 Bethesda Boulevard
Madison, WI 53704
608-390-1415 (w)
608-390-4478 (h)

OBJECTIVE   Position as a contract psychotherapist.

QUALIFICATIONS

ACSW

MSW Ohio State University

Group training program through American Association of Group Psychotherapists

Hypnotherapy training with Gill Boyne

Seventeen years' experience with adults and adolescents in individual, group and family therapy

EXPERIENCE

Provided therapy for over 400 patients in private practice.

Treated families of psychiatric inpatients as well as adult outpatients experiencing a variety of difficulties including depression, substance abuse, eating disorders, phobias, sexual dysfunction, and marriage and family breakdown.

Conducted inpatient and outpatient groups alone and with a psychiatrist or a psychiatric RN.

Provided therapy for groups and individuals undergoing emotional traumas related to divorce, relationships, life transition, identity crisis and loss.

Provided crisis intervention counseling for adults and adolescents undergoing emotional crises, many of whom were high suicide risks.

Provided counseling for families of children suffering from major and terminal illnesses.

Conducted groups for adolescent diabetes patients and families of nonambulatory mentally retarded adolescents.

Provided counseling for physically and mentally disabled adults and their families.

Patricia A. Gifford   **Page 2**

Provided therapy for medical inpatients and outpatients and their families facing issues of death and grief, high-risk pregnancy, and other social, emotional and economic issues related to acute and chronic illness.

Provided therapy for troubled adolescents and their families in residential treatment facility for adolescents.

EMPLOYMENT HISTORY

1987–present	Private practice
1986	Lead Social Worker, United Cerebral Palsy Association, Madison
1986	Certified Crisis Counselor, Suicide and Crisis Center, Madison
1983–86	Social Work Consultant, Deaf Smith County Home Health, Hereford, Texas
1980–83	Director, Center for Life Studies, Dallas
1973–78	Private practice with Psychiatrist, Dallas
1972–73	Director of Social Work, St. Paul Hospital, Dallas
1971–72	Medical Social Worker, Good Samaratian Hospital, St. Paul, Minnesota
1970–71	Student Field Placement, Children's Medical Center, Dayton, Ohio
1969–70	Student Field Placement, Children's Home, Cincinnati, Ohio

Freelance Resumes

Gail Taylor

Gail Taylor is working to become a professional voiceover specialist, commercial actress or books-on-tape reader. She is affiliated with the Thorton Agency and has been chosen for several parts. Note that she has included personal data generally not appropriate in a resume. Acting is one of the few professions where height, weight, and so forth, are considered BFOQ's—bona fide occupational qualifications. Therefore, casting directors would consider it strange if she didn't mention these facts.

GAIL TAYLOR

Thornton Agency
4800 Blanc Avenue
Parkville, WV 26505

304-822-8890
S.S. 573-20-1993

Height: 5'
Weight: 120

Hair: Brown
Eyes: Brown

Dress: Petite 10

TELEVISION

Job Search Series	Performer	Warner/Amex Cable, Dallas
10 O'Clock News	Weatherperson	Channel 4/15—WPTA-TV Parkersburg, WV
Broida's Stone Thomas Department Store	Fashion Commentator	WPTA-TV, Parkersburg, WV
Fairmont Food's Children's Show	Announcer/Performer	WPTA-TV, Parkersburg, WV
Greiner's Bakery	Commercial Performer	WPTA-TV, Parkersburg, WV

INDUSTRIAL

Live on Stage—The Drama of Accessories	Intro Announcer	Southwest Homefurnishings Association, Dallas
A Time to Remember	Ruth Hack/Bobbie B.	43rd Anniversary of Founding of AA in Dallas

STAGE

The People Next Door	Performer	NCCJ, Traveling Acting Company, Chicago
Pajama Game	Mable	West Virginia University
If Men Played Cards as Women Do	Director	West Virginia University
Death of a Salesman	Linda Loman	Carnegie Institute of Technology

TRAINING

Bachelor of Arts, Theater	West Virginia University
Theatre Major	Indiana University
Acting Major	Carnegie Institute of Technology
Presently, Vocal/Film Acting Coaching	Jeff Alexander
Commercial Acting	Kris Nicolau-Sharpley

SPECIAL SKILLS

Golf, Tennis, Swimming/Diving, Fencing, Singing, Ballroom Dancing, Piano and Body Mimicry.

Faith Quintavell

Faith started her career at a major metropolitan newspaper but soon decided that she preferred freelancing. Her resume spotlights both her client companies and successful projects in event planning, public relations, film production, writing, editing and desktop publishing. Her resume shows that she's the person to call if a firm needs to be promoted in print or through an event.

FAITH QUINTAVELL
16916 Canyon Road
Denton, NC 27615
704-633-0012

WORK EXPERIENCE

MANAGEMENT AND ORGANIZATION

- For **Philip Morris** managed five employees, coordinated and executed promotional events in nightclubs in Albuquerque, New Mexico.
- For the **New Music Seminar** prepared spreadsheets and tracked production budget.
- For **Gorilla Films** produced new sample reel including hiring new director for firm, overseeing artwork and directing edit sessions.
- Also for **Gorilla Films** was associate producer for Avon industrial shoot.
- For **various film production companies** served as a freelance production coordinator and production assistant.
- For **Lobsenz-Stevens Public Relations** garnered national magazine placements for client; was assistant event planner for press conference.
- For the **American Cancer Society** organized and publicized stop-smoking clinics and other events—won the Society's Most Innovative Public Education award, State of Connecticut, 1984.

WRITING AND EDITING

- For *B-Side Magazine* wrote article on rock group Bang Tango.
- As a **self-employed resume writer** wrote, edited and typeset clients' resumes.
- For **Aiken-Savitt Temporaries** wrote, edited and typeset word processing training manuals.
- For **Coopers & Lybrand, CPAs** wrote and edited desktop publishing manual for nationwide use.
- For **VH-1** music video channel conceived and wrote skits for video jock Jon Bauman.
- For **Lifetime Cable Television** answered fan mail.

Faith Quintavell   **Page 2**

WORD PROCESSING AND DESKTOP PUBLISHING

- For **Aiken-Savitt Temporaries** taught WordPerfect word processing.
- For **Artron Graphics** "laser set" resumes using Ventura desktop publishing.
- For **Coopers & Lybrand, CPAs** "laser set" business proposals using Mass-11 desktop publishing.

EMPLOYMENT HISTORY

Freelance Promotions Event Manager, Writer/Editor   March 1985–present
and Film & TV Production Coordinator/Assistant

Freelance Word Processor/Desktop Publisher   March 1985–present

Public Education Director   February 1984–February 1985
American Cancer Society, So. Fairfield County, CT

EDUCATION

BA with Honors in Psychology, University of North Carolina, 1983; GPA 3.45

INTERESTS

Avid rock music fan and record collector, amateur photographer and natural foods cook.

Resumes for Board or Committee Positions

People often need resumes for reasons other than paid work. For instance, before serving on a nonprofit board or committee, working in a high-profile position in a political campaign, giving a speech or applying for an award, you'll be asked to submit a resume summarizing your background and focusing on specific experience or interests relevant to the assignment in question.

If you were applying for a seat on the Park and Recreation Board of your city, you might mention that you coached softball for five years, managed the common grounds of your homeowners' association and spearheaded the effort to renovate the playground of your local elementary school. But if you were being considered for a director's position on your local United Way board, your resume would emphasize your myriad corporate contacts, ongoing volunteer work with a United Way affiliate, and knack for raising large amounts of money from companies and individuals.

In other words, a resume prepared for a volunteer assignment follows the same philosophy as one prepared for a paid position: It should be tailored for the job at hand. However, nonpaid experiences are likely to be more critical qualifications than employment histories.

Jo S. Zakas

Jo Zakas is an entrepreneur par excellence who has been asked to join numerous boards of directors, task forces, White House Conferences and so forth. The following resume serves her well in applying for a corporate or nonprofit board, a high-profile award for successful women, an executive office for a real estate trade group or a government appointment. Notice how her nonpaid activities take up the bulk of her resume, even though her business experience is listed at the top of the first page.

Now that we have discussed the main types of resume formats, let's look at how to use them effectively in situations many of us face during our careers:

- ☆ Applying for our first real job.
- ☆ Returning to the paid work force.
- ☆ Changing careers.
- ☆ Looking for a new position after many years in the work force or with one company.

Jo S. Zakas
4800 Westfield Road
Towning, KS 66614
913-797-3288

Jo Zakas began her entrepreneur career with the purchase of an insurance agency at the age of 17.

Business Experience

From 1972 to the present—Zakas developed and owns Clifton Square, a theme shopping center in Wichita, Kansas. She concluded the financing, purchasing, zoning, construction, leasing and management.

1964 to present—President and owner of Plaza Nine Ltd., whose involvements included retail fashion shops located in Kansas City, St. Louis and Wichita from 1964 to 1975; a Wichita restaurant operation from 1979 to 1981 and various real estate transactions in Kansas and Colorado; Communique Management Systems from 1989 to 1990, a management development system with offices in Newport Beach, California, and Wichita.

1960 to 1964—Greenwell Insurance Agency, Inc. Served as Vice President, General Agent and Broker, licensed in Missouri and Kansas. Budget Incorporated, a premium finance company for insurance, also owned and operated by Zakas.

1982–1985, a founder and the CEO of KSAS TV 24, independent station in Wichita, testified before the FCC in Washington, DC, during the licensing hearings.

1991—Talk Show Host—"Special Edition" KNSS 1240 Newstalk Radio.

Boards of Directors

Jo Zakas has served on the State Banking Board, State of Kansas (first woman to serve, first nonbanker to hold the Chairman of the Board), served two terms;
The Wichitan Publishing Co. (also served as President and CEO);
Small Business Administration, Wichita, Kansas;
Paul Revere Foundation; Kansas Good Roads Association;
National Conference of Christians and Jews; Wichita Area Chamber of Commerce;
Sales and Marketing Executive; Dimensions 100; Unlimited Investment Group of Wichita;
AAA Automobile Club of Kansas; YMCA of Wichita.

Jo S. Zakas **Page 2**

Appointments

Zakas served a Military Affairs Committee Vice Chairman, McConnell Air Force Base, Wichita Area Chamber of Commerce.

Served on the Task Force on Cost Effective Management and the Overall Economic Development Committee for the City of Wichita.

1992 Miss USA Judges Chair—Wichita Convention and Visitors Bureau.

Special Honors

In 1977, Zakas conferred with General Hill, 8th Air Force, Barksdale Air Force Base, Louisiana, regarding women's role in the military.

In 1977, she addressed the MBA graduates, Tucks School of Business, at Dartmouth College, Hanover, New Hampshire, regarding small business and real estate development.

In 1979 and 1981, Zakas was also the Executive in Residence for the Tucks School of Business.

In 1980, she was a delegate to the White House Conference on Small Business.

In 1980, Zakas was awarded the "Women of Achievement Award" from Women in Communications.

In 1982, Zakas participated in the 47th Joint Civilian Orientation Conference, invited by The Honorable Caspar W. Weinberger, Secretary of Defense. She was one of three ever selected for this honor from the state of Kansas.

Jo S. Zakas is unmarried, no children, plays tennis and golf, loves travel, paints and collects sculpture.

"I'm afraid we don't have anything for you just now, but I'll be glad to forward your resume to our parent company."

9

Resumes for First-Time Job Seekers

Recent college and high-school graduates face a Catch-22 in starting their new careers. Employers typically want to hire people with experience, which first-time job seekers seldom have. Yet companies advertise entry-level positions that imply no experience is required.

What can a person with good educational credentials and little paid background do to overcome this dilemma? Actually, there are a number of viable vehicles for gaining expertise other than a full-time job.

Volunteer Work

Plenty of volunteer opportunities exist for young people to try both when school is in session and during summer and holiday vacations. A short list of examples might include:

☆ Tutoring low-income children.

☆ Desktop publishing for a church newsletter.

☆ Taping books for the blind.

☆ Coaching a softball team.

☆ Working on a political campaign.

☆ Finding resources for library customers.

☆ Organizing and conducting a fund-raising campaign to buy furniture for the local family shelter.

☆ Collecting food for an area food bank.

☆ Driving senior citizens around town or to the Senior Center.

☆ Talking and reading to children in the pediatric ward of the county hospital.

All these experiences demonstrate initiative, perseverance and the desire to be of service to others, characteristics that potential employers admire. They will also substitute for paid experience if you give them a place of honor on your resume.

A Variety of Useful Experience, Not Necessarily Paid

School Activities

Extracurricular activities get a positive nod from companies as well. If you have applied and been selected for a competitive university, you already know that recruiters weigh your time away from classes as heavily as your academic record. Employers hold a similar view. They know that extracurricular activities usually require leadership, responsibility, follow-through and a variety of other traits that are desirable in successful job candidates. If you have been active in any school-sponsored functions, don't hesitate to use them as experience. They look good on your resume and allow you to collect stellar references.

Hobbies

Listing hobbies on a resume is particularly effective if they relate to the job you want. For instance, if you build remote-control model cars in your spare time, and you aspire to be an automotive engineer, most employers would appreciate the connection between the two. Suppose you designed and made all your clothes. Couture firms on Seventh Avenue would find this ability extremely desirable.

If a hobby coincides with your career objective, discuss it in your Experience section. If it doesn't, put it on your resume anyway, but in a less prominent position.

Clubs

Club memberships can be useful, both because of the role you play and the organization's overall mission. Fraternities and sororities are good examples of this. They offer actives the opportunity to assume highly responsible positions quickly. Anyone who has been Chair of the Homecoming Celebration or the Alumni Fund Drive can take credit for a host of demonstrated skills, including team building, leadership, problem solving, mediation, creativity, resourcefulness, perseverance, organization and follow-through.

If your club is concerned primarily with issues similar to those of the company or organization you're pursuing, mentioning it will elicit a favorable response with hiring managers. For instance, if you have been active in the Audubon Society, and you are hoping to land a position with the EPA, your obvious interest in ecology will give you an edge over the competition.

As with school-sponsored extracurricular activities, clubs can be an important addition to your resume, even if their mission doesn't apply to your job objective. Serving as an officer or committee chair always impresses potential employers, unless they are looking for a candidate who wants a dead-end job.

Internships

Paid or unpaid internships are great ways to accumulate experience in a potential career field. Concurrent with deciding whether the career is right for you, you are compiling a list of achievements that will add sizzle to your resume. Since you're just beginning your career, interviewers can't expect you to come equipped with years of experience. But if they see that you spent a summer or a semester "trying on" your new career, they assume the odds are good that you'll be a happy, successful employee.

Even if your internship is in a different field than the one you want to work in, completing it shows that you are familiar with the world of work and able to conform to its culture and policies. Transferable skills can count for a lot when there isn't much employment history to discuss.

Part-Time Jobs

As long as the puritan work ethic is an honored philosophy in American business, part-time jobs held while in school or during vacations will be excellent selling points with employers, particularly if they relate to your chosen career. Working at McDonald's, in a clothing or grocery store, the school cafeteria or an office will count in your favor as well, especially if you mention your job helped to pay for personal or school expenses. Many of the people reading your resume had part-time jobs themselves, or are parents facing the daunting prospect of footing the bill for their children's college degree. When they read about your work-study regimen, they'll either identify with you or hope their offspring will have the good sense to be as motivated. Either way, you have made yourself a friend.

As you write about paid or unpaid experience, remember to discuss accomplishments, rather than duties, if possible. The following are some typical achievements from activities or part-time job experience:

☆ Revised the database for the Leadership Dallas Alumni Yearbook.

☆ Authored a 24-chapter manual on the use of surf boats in lifeguarding.

☆ Carried diverse client caseload in terms of ethnicity, age and social class.

☆ Wrote personal letters for President Bush's political liaison and participated in planning and executing large mailings to up to 1,500 constituents.

☆ Gathered and organized tourism-related information to assist staff and guests in a newly opened, 40-room upscale bed-and-breakfast inn.

☆ Worked on a Homecoming committee that designed and built the Grand Prize float for Texas Tech, called "ET Phone Home."

While your achievements may not have the scope of a Nobel Prize winner (or even of your parents), anything you can do to spotlight a unique contribution will capture recruiters' attention and set you apart from the hundreds of business-as-usual candidates they hear from every week.

Education

While most resume writers emphasize experience over education, graduates with highly prized degrees from prestigious universities may want to list their educational credentials first. Before you construct your resume, check with your college placement office to find out if many employers regularly recruit and hire graduates from your school. If they do, give your degree(s) a place of honor at the top of your first page, and list your part-time jobs and activities below it. You may also want to emphasize your education if your career requires a specific credential, such as an RN (nursing), an MSW (clinical social work), or a BSEE (electrical engineering). On the other hand, if your specific degree isn't essential for the position you seek, feature your experience as your most marketable asset.

Your education section should include the same types of entries as the ones discussed in Chapter 4. Because a college degree is your most important educational credential to date, it should be listed at the top of your resume as follows:

B.S. in Psychology, University of San Francisco, 1994

You can also list your GPA and number of semesters on the Dean's List, and note that you graduated magna cum laude.

Because many employers now look for multifaceted graduates, be sure to note a strong minor or a certificate in a given subject area. This approach is especially appropriate if your major field is not in great demand.

Continuing education classes in computer skills, foreign languages or other subjects that enhance your marketability also serve a useful purpose on your resume. Don't neglect to include study-abroad programs, extensive travel and other mind-expanding experiences. Most employers view these as bona fide educational background, even if you didn't receive credit for them.

Honors and Awards

Be sure to mention if you were chosen for *Who's Who in Colleges and Universities,* Mortarboard, Phi Beta Kappa or Speechmaker of the Year, or earned other kudos based on your activities or academics.

Personal or Other Facts

Finally, at the bottom of your resume, mention hobbies that aren't related to your job objective, and any other personal data a potential employer might find useful. But don't include your age, weight, health or other personal facts that frankly are none of his business.

References

You probably have been advised about the importance of having good references to provide potential employers. To be sure, it's wise to have a list of people who'll say wonderful things about you. However, it's not wise to include them on your resume.

Unless you've volunteered or worked with a well-known, admired person, you'll just be wasting resume space by listing references' names, addresses and phone numbers. The same is true for the phrase, "References Available Upon Request," since prospective employers assume you'll provide them with the names of instructors, advisers, managers, fellow volunteers and other reliable sources that they can call about your abilities.

As you work on your resume, call favorite professors and other advocates to ascertain if they'll give you a good recommendation. Be sure to double-check their addresses and phone numbers and the correct spelling of their names. Then, list them on a separate sheet to give to employers who request references.

By the way, if an employer bothers to ask for references, you're a leading candidate for the position. After giving the employer the list, alert each reference that they may receive a call and explain any issues that are likely to be mentioned. This way, your advocates will be primed to spotlight your skills, personality traits and relevant activities when the employer calls.

Two Resumes, One Student

Harold Buck

Harry Buck sent two resumes: one that resulted in a position as Research Assistant in Biostatistics at Penn State, and the other that targets a teaching job after completion of his Master's degree at the University of Minnesota. Both are excellent examples of how to make the most of part-time experience and related education.

The Research Assistant Resume

Harold Miller Buck

Before 6/1/93
818 Ranchita Road SE #302
Minneapolis, MN 55427
612-441-7239

After 6/1/93
39 Straighten Lane
Lexington, PA 15146
412-503-3912/412-834-2474

Employment Objective   An entry-level position as a statistical consultant.

Education   MS, University of Minnesota, 1992
Major in Statistics with minor in Operations Management Science (3.7 GPA).

BA, University of Chicago, 1990
Double major in Statistics and Pure Mathematics. Graduated with honors.

Employment

1990–Present   UNIVERSITY OF MINNESOTA

Statistical Consultant (1992–Present)

Assisted University students, faculty and staff with the application of statistical methods to research in the natural and social sciences. Designed experiments, taught clients how to interpret results, suggested analysis strategies and analyzed data. Collaborated with experienced consultants on difficult problems.

Teaching Assistant (1990–1991)

Conducted problem sessions and office hours for undergraduate and graduate statistics courses. Graded tests/homework and provided timely and lucid solutions.

1985–Present   LONG BEACH TOWNSHIP BEACH PATROL

Consultant (1990–Present)

Authored a 24-chapter manual on the use of surf boats in lifeguarding and another manual on other aspects of patrol operation. Designed a set of more than 20 forms that streamlined record keeping and were instrumental in protecting the township from lawsuits. Conducted a statistical investigation on ocean rescues over a 3-year period to provide management with a basis for intelligent allocation of manpower. Planned the acquisition of a computer system to assist in the management of patrol operations and directed implementation and training.

Harold Miller Buck   **Page 2**

<u>Lieutenant</u> (1988–1989, summer only)

Trained and supervised 25 lifeguards. Managed $50,000 in equipment and 1.5 miles of ocean beach. Enforced local ordinances and practiced public relations.

<u>Lifeguard</u> (1985–1988, summer only)

Guarded 400 yards of ocean beach. Rescued 19 swimmers and boaters.

Qualifications   <u>Coursework</u>: Linear and nonlinear experimental design (including response surface design and Taguchi methods), advanced simulation analysis and statistical computing, quality assurance, linear regression, nonparametric statistics, categorical data, stochastic processes, multivariate analysis, survey design, mathematical statistics and probability, consulting, operations management.

<u>Computing Packages</u>: S, Minitab, MacAnova, GLIM, Mathematica, SIMAN. (Willing to learn SAS, SPSS, and/or other packages.)

<u>Computing Languages</u>: FORTRAN, Pascal, BASIC; learning C and Lisp.

References   Excellent academic and professional references available upon request.

The High School Math Teacher Resume

Harold Miller Buck
822 41st Ave #487
St. Paul, MN 55121
612-784-1736

Employment Objective

A position as a high school mathematics instructor.

Education

MS in Mathematics, University of Minnesota, expected June 1993

MS in Statistics, University of Minnesota, 1992

BA, University of Chicago, 1990
Double major in Statistics and Pure Mathematics. Graduated with honors.

Qualifications

<u>Teaching</u>: Seven years of experience working as a grader, tutor, teaching assistant and teacher; participation in numerous teaching workshops and seminars offered through the University of Minnesota; independent reading on teaching techniques.

<u>Coursework</u>: Calculus; real and complex analysis; linear and abstract algebra; applied and mathematical statistics; measure theory and probability; optimization; numerical analysis; simulation. Programming in Pascal, FORTRAN, BASIC and Mathematica.

<u>Coaching</u>: Experience coaching team and individual sports. Proficiency in cross country running, swimming, fencing, ultimate frisbee, chess, and other sports; some experience with lacrosse, soccer and football. First aid and CPR certification.

Employment 1990–1993

<u>UNIVERSITY OF MINNESOTA</u>

<u>Teaching Assistant</u> (1990–1991, 1991–1993)
Conducted problem sessions and office hours for undergraduate and graduate statistics and operations/management science courses. Constructed tests and quizzes, graded tests and homework and provided timely and lucid solution sets.

Harold Miller Buck   Page 2

                 <u>Statistical Consultant</u> (1992)

                 Assisted University students, faculty, and staff with the application of statistics to research in the natural and social sciences. Designed experiments, taught clients how to interpret results, suggested analysis strategies and analyzed data.

1985–Present   LONG BEACH TOWNSHIP BEACH PATROL

                 <u>Instructor/Consultant</u> (1990–Present)

                 Instructor for Ocean Lifeguard Training Course. Provided individual coaching in rowing and swimming. Authored a manual for the use of surf boats in lifeguarding. Organized and directed competitions for junior lifeguards. Designed forms and conducted statistical analyses. Editor for U.S. Lifesaving Association magazine.

                 <u>Lieutenant</u> (1988–1989, summer only)

                 Trained and supervised 25 lifeguards. Managed $50,000 in equipment and 1.5 miles of ocean beach. Enforced local ordinances and practiced public relations.

                 <u>Lifeguard</u> (1985–1988, summer only)

1990–1991   PENNSYLVANIA STATE UNIVERSITY

                 <u>Research Assistant in Biostatistics</u>

                 Collaborated with medical researchers by designing and analyzing experiments. Taught introductory biostatistics course for first-year medical students. Presented paper at 1991 Biometric Society conference in Houston.

Success Stories

Amber Frantz

Amber wrote this resume as a sales tool to help her land a meaty summer job that would pay better than McDonald's and offer impressive resume credentials after she graduated from Northwestern. Because she knows her alma mater has an excellent reputation in the business community, she put her education at the top. She also listed her major, minor and various certificates, which show her commitment to being a well-rounded student. Amber is deservedly proud of her high school and college grades, so she has included her GPAs as well.

Her internship with the Greater Dallas Chamber was unpaid, but she received credit from her high school for the assignment. Because this program is highly competitive, interns generally participate in meaningful projects that are impressive when listed on their resumes. As you can see, this is true in Amber's case.

The numerous activities she participated in and awards she won round out her story.

Amber is currently employed during the summer at Cyrix, a company that designs microprocessors. She is serving as a personnel generalist, working on a variety of projects, including an employee handbook, human resources database, new-hire orientation program, and information and referral system. Her contacts and resume got her the job.

Amber Frantz
7646 Mustang Drive
Farmers Branch, TX 75253
214-139-1162

Education

Sophomore, Northwestern University
Communications major with political science concentration/business
institutions and leadership certificates
GPA: 3.58

Advanced honors graduate of J.J. Pearce High School, 14 in a class of 530,
95.7 GPA.

Experience

*Intern-Leadership Development Department, Greater Dallas Chamber of
Commerce, January 1991–May 1991*

- Revised and promoted the Leadership Appointment Program that
  matches community leaders with nonprofit boards.
  - Designed a survey to get input from nonprofit organizations.
  - Developed and implemented a direct-mail campaign.
  - Reformatted system to incorporate results of the survey.
- Attended meetings of the Dallas Alliance.
- Represented the Chamber at a Texas Research League meeting for
  school finance.
- Revised database for the Leadership Dallas Alumni Yearbook.
- Confirmed speakers for Leadership Dallas and Opportunity Dallas.

Sales Associate at Jay Jacobs, July 1991–September 1991, December 1991

Interim Office Manager, Dimensions Associates, Summers of 1987–1989

- Answered phones, made weekly deposits, typed newspaper columns, put
  together newsletter bulk mail, put together seminar workbooks, collated
  data from 1,000 surveys on single lifestyle issues, scheduled client
  appointments, promoted workshops.

Familiar with Wordperfect, Microsoft Word, PFS Write and Deskmate Plus
on IBM personal computers; and Microsoft Word on the Macintosh.

Amber Frantz   Page 2

Activities

Northwestern University
- Shepard Dorm First Floor Representative.
- Literacy Tutor for Adults.
- Pledge Class President, Delta Zeta.

J.J. Pearce High School
- Selected as one of 12 Richardson Independent School District students to participate in a cultural exchange with students from Oyama, Japan, via live teleconference sponsored by Fujitsu America.
- Chosen to represent Pearce High School at monthly meetings with school district administrators to discuss issues such as racial tensions and school finance.
- Served as Student Council officer.
- Elected Students Against Drunk Driving president.
- Played on school volleyball team, six years.
- Other activities include Pre-law Club, Interact Service Club and the Pearce Literary Magazine.

Honors

National Merit Finalist
Who's Who at J.J. Pearce
Who's Who of American High School Students
Raider Award (leadership, citizenship, excellence in academics and athletics)
National Honor Society
Spanish Honor Society

Other Good Resumes

This section provides some other excellent resumes from beginning professionals around the country.

SAMANTHA JO HAUSER
9021 Ellis Drive   —   Dune, SC 29575   —   803-877-9437

OBJECTIVE

To obtain a position in public relations or special event management involving the planning and organization of events, preparation of publicity pieces and publication of materials.

EDUCATION

Emory University, Atlanta, GA, GPA 3.3/4.0—Bachelor of Arts in Psychology, May 1992
    Honors: Dean's List—five semesters
    Activities: Delta Phi Epsilon sorority—Rush Day Head, Initiation Brunch 1990 and Formal 1992
    Chairperson; Residence Hall Association—Activities Chairperson; Student Host; Tutor for Second-Grade students; Mademoiselle College Marketing Board; involved with PRSSA.

EXPERIENCE

Development Assistant, June 1992–present
Delaware Valley Friends School, Bryn Mawr, PA

- Write and publish monthly newsletter to 300 constituents and contribute to biannual newsletter to 2,000 constituents.
- Planned school events including 1st Annual Alumni Day, Professional Open Houses, All-School Picnic, Donor Breakfast, Founders' Day, Auction and Golf Tournament.
- Conduct monthly open house tours and handled admission inquiries.
- Help design invitations to events and other printed materials.
- Created 1992–1993 development plan and compile monthly development activity report.
- Maintain database of 2,000 constituents and donors and all gifts received by school.

Career Assistant, January 1990–May 1992
Emory University Career Planning and Placement Center, Atlanta GA

- Managed publicity and reception for Career Day 1990, International and Environmental Careers Forums.

SAMANTHA JO HAUSER   Page Two

— Interviewed and trained new Career Assistants.
— Advised students and alumni throughout the University and created outreach career programs.
— Established database for the Alumni Career Network providing access to career contacts and networking opportunities.

Communications Intern, Summer 1991
Philadelphia Convention and Visitors Bureau, Philadelphia, PA

— Wrote press releases and mediawires. Contacted press for various festivals and events.
— Aided in the organization of event previews, press conferences, photo shoots and membership meetings.
— Prepared information for bureau publications.
— Represented the bureau at several press receptions.

Public Relations Assistant, Fall Semester 1990
Emory University Museum of Art and Archaeology, Atlanta, GA

— Aided director in compiling press kits and media lists.
— Helped coordinate and oversee festivals and opening ceremonies of exhibits and handled press inquiries.

Public Relations Intern, Summer 1990
Earle Palmer Brown and Spiro, Philadelphia, PA

— Assisted Account Executives on several accounts, primarily Donnelley Directory.
— Researched information and wrote for three client newsletters.
— Organized and compiled materials for client presentations and edited press releases.

ADDITIONAL INFORMATION

Fluency in WordPerfect, MacWrite, Microsoft Works and PageMaker applications. Have extensive international travel. Studied French for eight years.

Sarah Patel
21090 Castaldian Road
Chesterview, NJ 08753
609-734-5383

EDUCATION

University of Arizona, Tucson, AZ
Bachelor of Science in Family Studies, December 1991
Emphasis: Psychology and Sociology

EXPERIENCE

Phone Counselor, Contact Dallas

- In training program to become a crisis intervention counselor for this community hot line.

Associated Students of the University of Arizona

Panhellenic Rush Counselor

- Conducted daily meetings on rush procedures. Attended a for-credit course and a retreat to develop leadership and counseling skills.
- Encouraged girls to keep an open mind. Counseled those with problems or disappointments.

Eating Advocacy Team Member

- Assisted student health services in prevention and aid for students with eating disorders.

APEX Member

- Promoted and encouraged higher education for high school students.

Spring Fling Supply Staff

- Assisted in production of largest student-run carnival in United States.

Alpha Epsilon Phi Sorority

Assistant Pledge Trainer

- Selected to assist the pledge trainer in all areas of pledge training. Matched pledges with actives and developed activities to build their rapport.

Standards Board Committee
- Monitored the behavior of actives and pledges, and offered praise and constructive suggestions for improvement as needed.

Homecoming Committee—2-year participant
Liaison Committee—Alumni contact via newsletter
Block Party Philanthropy—Fund-raising activity
Spring Fling Committee—2-year participant

EMPLOYMENT

Temporary Work, Venson & Associates—3/92 to Present
Server Support, Macaroni Grill—12/91 to 3/92
Sales Representative, Primrose—6/91 to 8/91
- Received incentive awards for high sales volume in ladies' boutique, catering to upscale clientele.
- Provided customer service for independent store in sales of trend-setting and designer clothing.

Hostess, Applebees' Restaurant—6/88 to 8/88
- Seated patrons and assisted wait staff in service of casual dining fare for restaurant seating 100.

"Try not to be discouraged . . . not everyone can write their complete autobiography on a single sheet of paper."

10

Resumes for Women Returning to the Paid Workforce

O ne of the most important concepts for women returning to the workforce to remember is that their years of experience count for something in the paid work world. Such activities include the following:

☆ Doing volunteer work.
☆ Juggling schedules.
☆ Counseling friends and family members.
☆ Giving birthday and dinner parties.

☆ Averting and resolving crises.

☆ Making important buying decisions.

☆ Mediating disputes.

☆ Planning family vacations.

☆ Advocating and supporting causes.

☆ Developing and stretching budgets.

☆ Solving problems creatively.

☆ Redecorating houses.

☆ Coordinating thousand-mile relocations.

☆ Running an information and referral network.

☆ Challenging, shaping and nurturing young minds.

☆ Maintaining a sense of humor when everyone else is preaching doom and gloom.

While such women may not be as marketable as professionals who haven't interrupted their careers to focus on family responsibilities, they certainly have more to offer than someone right out of school. Life experience alone gives these women a host of opportunities to deal with situations not yet encountered by career neophytes.

Unfortunately, in determining their worth to the business world, reentry women may be their own greatest detractors. Unless a homemaker believes she should be compensated for her work, it will be hard to convince her that anyone else will pay her for it. After all, no one has offered her any money for her efforts to date. How can she logically assume she's now a valuable commodity just because she decided to return to the workforce? Changing this mind-set represents at least 50 percent of the process of transforming a homemaker into a paid professional. If she recognizes her worth, other people will, too. If she continues to think work is its own reward, or that she has few skills an employer would need or want, others will tend to agree with her. Her assumption becomes her reality!

If you are a homemaker having difficulty believing you have marketable achievements, go back to Chapter 2 and rate yourself against the skills inventory. This exercise is designed to help job seekers use both their paid and nonpaid experiences as raw material for their resumes. As noted in both Chapters 2 and 9, experience is valuable regardless of whether it commands a fee. You may be surprised by the number and variety of things you have done that require an abundance of transferable skills. People in other settings get paid for using those skills. Why shouldn't you?

To facilitate the transformation of nonpaid accomplishments into an effective resume, let's look at some typical areas of your life where applicable achievements abound.

Volunteer Experience

Annette Strauss is currently in charge of a national task force to examine and make recommendations to stabilize and nurture the American urban family. About two weeks before President Clinton chose her for this position, she finished two terms as mayor of the city of Dallas, where she had also served as a city councilwoman. What led Annette Strauss to seek political office? What gave her the visibility and credibility throughout the city to mount a successful campaign for election as Dallas's first female mayor? Her volunteer work.

Carol Schlipak is foundation director as well as director of development for a large urban county community college district. The chancellor of the district personally asked her to assume this dual role because of her outstanding success in raising funds for the local League of Women Voters.

Patti Clapp is vice president of education and governmental affairs for her city's Chamber of Commerce. Before joining the chamber, Patti hadn't held a paid job for a number of years. What convinced a group of high-profile business leaders to hire her instead of one of the many other qualified candidates who applied? Her volunteer leadership in her children's school district and with various other nonprofit organizations that seek to enhance opportunities for women and children in the community.

While your volunteer background may not qualify you to be mayor, it can be an excellent source of relevant experience for your resume. The following are a few examples of volunteer achievements that are transferable to many paid positions:

☆ Serving as an officer or committee chair for your local PTA.

☆ Chairing the social or governmental affairs committee of your homeowners' association.

☆ Coordinating the fund-raising bazaar for your church.

☆ Being a Big Sister to a troubled or disadvantaged youth.

☆ Teaching an adult to read.

☆ Organizing a local campaign to put a park in your neighborhood or a stoplight at a busy intersection.

☆ Designing and producing your club newsletter.

☆ Working with the senior class to plan an all-night event after graduation.

☆ Planning the monthly programs for your sorority alumnae club.

☆ Writing and gathering names for a petition to start a high school softball program for girls.

☆ Working on a political campaign.

☆ Doing crisis counseling for a mental-health hot line.

☆ Serving on a task force to fulfill site-based management requirements for your child's school.

The list of possibilities is endless. The point is that you deserve credit for the bona fide work you have done for your child's school, community, favorite social service agency, church, fraternal or social organization, volunteer league or alumni association.

Hobbies

Hobbies are another source of experience to include on your resume, especially if they are related to your job objective. For instance, if you have become a semiprofessional flower arranger, mention this when you apply for a job in a flower shop. If you love to give dinner parties and help friends plan their children's weddings or graduation celebrations, you could be a very valuable addition to a catering or event-planning firm.

Hobbies increase your knowledge of a specific subject. They give you on-the-job training and a level of expertise in areas that relatively few people may possess. Consider Debbie Fields of Mrs. Field's cookies. She turned her recipe for chocolate chip cookies into a multimillion-dollar enterprise.

Just as you did with your volunteer experience, examine your hobbies carefully to extract the skills that apply to your new profession. Whether you have been paid to use them isn't nearly as important as how well you sell them on paper and in person.

Hobbies are incredibly diverse, but here's a short list of activities that many homemakers have turned into paid careers:

☆ Cooking.

☆ Interior design.

☆ Party planning.

☆ Organizing closets, work spaces or kitchen cabinets.

☆ Making clothes for adults, children and even pets.

☆ Planning vacations.

☆ Reading.

☆ Collecting cookbooks, antiques, depression glass, etc.

☆ Exercising.

☆ Gardening.

☆ Writing articles, stories or books.

☆ Breeding purebred animals.

Do some brainstorming about how your hobbies might relate to your work. You may be surprised at some of the correlations.

Also think about paid work you may have done before you decided to become a full-time homemaker. Teaching is a good example of a career in which the basic skills haven't changed substantially over the years. While you may want to take a few courses to brush up on some new learning techniques, the process of imparting knowledge to young minds isn't radically different than it was 10 years ago. If you were a good teacher then, you're likely to be a good teacher now.

To give yourself maximum credit for skills that continue to be relevant after a number of years, use a functional resume format instead of a chronological one. Attaching dates to job titles automatically prioritizes them because it's assumed that recent experience is more important than more dated credentials. The assumption that expertise decreases with time makes sense if you are dealing with such highly technical subjects as computer programming, electrical engineering or heart surgery. But it doesn't hold true with all careers. For instance, customer service skills haven't changed much either. No doubt the follow-up techniques you used 15 years ago will work just as well today, except you will probably rely on a computer instead of a Day-Timer to generate your tickler file. Hence, you should list your relevant skills without attaching dates to them.

After experience, education will probably be the next most important resume category. Use the Education section in Chapter 4 as your guide. If you have taken some catchup courses or boast a newly minted degree that's relevant to your job objective, give your academic background a prominent place on your resume. Fresh credentials are always a powerful selling point.

Success Stories

This section provides some excellent examples of resumes submitted by women who successfully returned to the paid workforce.

Nury Reichert

Nury Reichert is a good example of a homemaker who used her volunteer experience, marketing and public relations background to move into a paid position after 22 years of raising children and working in her husband's business. She writes, "When I felt I needed a change to establish my own identity, I prepared the enclosed resume. It helped me land the best job of my life as executive director of a small nonprofit organization attached to the University of Pennsylvania: The Global Interdependence Center, from which I recently retired, at my request, after six wonderful and productive years.

"At the first board meeting, several directors commented on what they liked about me as expressed in the resume. One mentioned my openness about having been a housewife for 13 years and another liked my assessment of 'common sense.'"

nury reichert

17 CHEROKEE PLACE
PHILADELPHIA, PA 19140
215-827-3899

CAREER OBJECTIVE

Although born in Spain and raised in Venezuela, I have lived in Philadelphia since 1958. My children were born here, benefited from public education and I have a deep appreciation for the enduring values alive in this city. As an educated woman, with strong business and communication skills, I would like to contribute to make Philadelphia a city that works well and is justly recognized by businesses and individuals as the most livable city in America.

EXPERIENCE

1974–83   Marketing Partner
REICHERT-FACILIDES ASSOCIATES PC

Created a marketing and Public Relations role in 8-person architecture and city planning firm:

Developed marketing plan: analyzed firm's past performance in its major market segments, evaluated prospective markets and assisted partners in establishing long and short-term tactical goals.

Gathered information about prospective jobs, analyzed to determine specific issues, coordinated and prepared proposal response and assisted partners in interview preparation, including writing and editing of speeches, proposals and correspondence.

Directed public relations efforts including partners contacts with prospective leads. Coordinated awards entries, wrote and placed press releases, visited editors.

Developed and maintained marketing information systems.

The firm doubled in size and revenues during my tenure.

1979–83   Partner
HOMEWORKS: Bought and rehabilitated houses in Germantown.

1961–74   Raised a family.

1958–60   Research Editor: The Saturday Evening Post.

1957   Editor: The Greater Boston Shopper.

nury reichert

MEMBERSHIPS AND CIVIC INVOLVEMENT

American Association of University Women—Chair, 39th Annual Fall Conference: "Women in the Third World"

Committee on City Policy

Society for Marketing Professional Services—Past Board Member, Greater Delaware Valley Chapter

United Way—Past Committee Member and Trustee

Philadelphia Bar Association—Member, Fee Dispute Committee

Philadelphia: Past, Present, and Future—Member, International City Task Force

Health Systems Agency—Past Board Member, Northwest SAC

Citizen's Committee on Public Education—Past Board Member

Bicentennial Women's Center—Founding and Board Member

Save the Wissahickon Committee—Cofounder

Upper Roxborough Civic Association—Cofounder

Barnard College—Pennsylvania Regional Representative

Columbia University Club of Philadelphia—Member, Executive Committee

Designing Women—Charter Member and Past Vice President

Delaware Valley Montessori Association—Past Delegate and Treasurer

SKILLS

Languages: Fluent in Spanish. Working knowledge of French, Catalan, and German.

Managerial: Strong verbal and writing skills. Self-starter, able and willing to organize and coordinate activities and work under pressure. Common sense.

Paige Louise Minsky

Paige Minsky was the consummate professional volunteer, holding several leadership roles in community organizations. Of all the projects she spearheaded, she particularly enjoyed those that involved the welfare of children. As her own children grew older, she decided to seek a paid position that would use her expertise and contacts developed during 12 years of nonprofit service.

One of the organizations she applied to was the Anti-Defamation League. When it realized that a professional with an extensive background in diversity issues was available, it quickly hired Paige to manage a new "A World of Difference" program, which teaches children the intrinsic benefits of our country's blend of cultures.

Now Paige is ready to take her message on diversity to corporations. She is using the following resume to sell herself to business executives. Notice how she combines her paid and unpaid experience to illustrate the depth of her expertise.

PAIGE LOUISE MINSKY
17181 Park Hill Drive
San Antonio, TX 78239
512-702-3774

OBJECTIVE

Seeking a challenging and responsible position in Community Relations/Diversity
Management in the public or private sector.

PERSONAL QUALIFICATIONS

- Fifteen years of increasing responsibility in nonprofit management in areas of
  diversity, community education and awareness.
- Expert in volunteer management and recruitment.
- Heavy background in public relations for the public sector.
- Experience in planning and coordinating special events.
- Extensive work in public schools as an educator in special program areas.
- A change agent, comfortable in developing new programs.
- Strong problem-solving skills particularly in identifying options and resources.
- Skilled in communicating with people in a variety of roles from corporate CEOs
  to teachers and their students.

EMPLOYMENT

Assistant Regional Director   Anti-Defamation League   1989–present

Community Relations Programming

- Staff "A World of Difference" and relate its message to corporate and public
  sector. This program has been presented to over 2,000 teachers in the metroplex.
- Effectively communicate with the media on a wide range of issues.
- Serve as liaison including meeting with and speaking to community groups such as
  schools and civic organizations, religious institutions and area businesses.
- Initiate and mentor young leadership group and plan ongoing programs.
- Staff committees including fund-raising, legal affairs and program.
- Develop and maintain relations with volunteer board to promote ADL program.

Fund-raising:

- Organize direct solicitations including planning and executing fund-raising events
  that gross $400,000 per year.

Paige Louise Minsky   **Page Two**

Problem Solving

- Troubleshoot for individuals regarding diversity issues.
- Manage information and referral activities.
- Investigate discrimination complaints.

Writing/Editing

- Create and edit newsletters, press releases, speeches, promotional and thank-you letters.
- Write reports documenting organization activities.

SIGNIFICANT COMMUNITY EXPERIENCE

- Vice President for volunteers, Hamilton Park Elementary School (the only magnet school in the Richardson School District)
- Program Co-Chair, Community Board Institute
- Board of Directors, Temple Emanu-El
- Chairman, Celebrations Committee, Temple Emanu-El
- Volunteer Teacher, National Council of Jewish Women, "Hello Israel"
- Recording Secretary, National Council of Jewish Women

EDUCATION

    University of Texas at Austin
    Bachelor of Arts with double major in Political Science and History

Other Good Resumes

Rebekah A. Taylorson
14 Sawgrass Boulevard
Ponte Vedra, FL 33138
305-250-8887

OBJECTIVE   Position in public or community relations, especially in event and/or program planning where project management, volunteer coordination, development and knowledge of community resources would be useful.

APPLICABLE EXPERIENCE

Chaired the March of Dimes campaign for the City of Ponte Vedra, 1982–83. Coordinated neighborhood and local volunteer organizations. Contributions increased 29% over previous year.

Served on the Highland Park United Methodist Church solicitations committee for 1988 Wesley-Rankin Community Center auction. Asked for donations and filled tables. Raised $47,000. (Wesley-Rankin Center does community outreach in Ponte Vedra. It teaches women to be self-sufficient, provides day care, scouting, and sports activities for low-income families.)

Coordinated volunteer efforts as President of the Ponte Vedra County Alumnae Panhellenic to interest young women in attending college and joining a sorority. Planned a fund-raiser that brought in 500% of 1986's proceeds. Organized the annual tea and high school visits to recruit young women and their mothers. Invited to attend many key civic functions in the Ponte Vedra area as a result of this position.

Worked on development activities for the Ronald McDonald House in St. Petersburg, including the Fantasy Forest (an annual holiday train exhibit), yearly fashion shows and a Mardi Gras party.

Active member of First United Methodist Church in Ponte Vedra for the past 10 years, serving in these capacities:

1989 Membership Chair. Coordinate volunteers who recruit new members by visitation, marketing and planned church activities. Keep track of current membership data.

Rebekah A. Taylorson   page 2

1984–87 President, Rachel Group (United Methodist Women). Planned and scheduled monthly meetings and served as liaison between the group, UMW and the Church board.

1988 Member, Worship Committee Coordinated all greeters for weekly services.

1986–88 Member, Pastor-Parish Relations Committee. Took an active role in this human resources committee, which evaluates and recommends salaries, ministerial placement, congregation/staff relations etc.

OTHER COMMITTEE INVOLVEMENT

Chair, Neighborhood Crime Watch
Delivery Committee, Meals on Wheels
Ponte Vedra County Friends of the Library
Presbyterian Hospital of Ponte Vedra Auxiliary
Ponte Vedra P.T.A.

EMPLOYMENT

Bookkeeper in husband's dental practice for past 10 years.
Loan Processor, Fox and Jacobs Credit Union
Financial Planner, Fox and Jacobs
Senior Payroll Clerk, Enserch Corporation
Teller, St. Petersburg National Bank

EDUCATION

BBA Florida Tech University, 1974

Continuing Education:

Marketing and Practice Management Seminars, with my husband and staff in Banff, Canada; Hilton Head, SC; Phoenix, AZ; and Dallas, TX. These seminars focus on marketing and management skills, self-motivation, financial planning and income analysis. I am very involved in the overall decision making of my husband's dental practice.

Nicole Dorsey

3321 Redbird   Dallas, Texas 75205   214-238-7355

OBJECTIVE

Entry-level position in computer programming that provides an opportunity to use my skills and experience and offers a challenging and stimulating environment.

PERSONAL QUALIFICATIONS

- Capacity to learn quickly and use newfound knowledge concisely and accurately.
- Broad-based understanding of basic business principles and applications.
- Facility for talking with people at all organizational levels.
- High commitment to getting the job done right.
- Delight in new techniques and concepts.

EDUCATION

BS in Math, Computer Science Option, UTA, GPA: 3.57

APPLICABLE COURSEWORK

- Created programs to set up and maintain files for database management.
- Wrote programs to access various types of sequential and linked list files.
- Designed a program to implement a two-pass assembler and direct linking loader.
- Developed an interactive program to play "move the mouse through the maze."
- Utilized programs to analyze and predict outcomes of statistical models.
- Used FORTRAN, PL/I, SAS, Data General Nova, and Assembly languages in conjunction with the IBM 4341, Tektronix, DEC 20, and PDP-11 hardware.
- Have six credits in general accounting techniques and practices.

EXPERIENCE

Tutor, for high school students in programming, geometry, and algebra, 1984 to present

Junior League of Dallas, 1983 to present

- In charge of inventory, ledgers, sales, money, setting up, dismantling, and redistribution of goods at Senior Citizens' Craft Fair.
- Helped design and sew costumes for the annual fund raising ball.

General American Oil, 1977–1978
Promoted to production clerk.

- Maintained oil production ledgers for company's entire output of over 200 wells.
- Developed graphic reports of production capabilities for designated wells.
- Managed records for production reports on both wholly and consortium owned properties.

Office "Jack of All Trades" including PBX and telex operator.

PERSONAL

Hobbies include tennis, sewing, and reading.

11

Resumes for Career Changers

While it may seem paradoxical, career changers and homemakers share similar concerns about their marketability. Both worry about their ability to compete with other candidates in their newly chosen fields. Both are afraid they'll have to start at the bottom, as though they were novice job seekers. And both tend to belittle their overall experience while magnifying their lack of knowledge of a particular subject. In assessing their worth to prospective employers, they often give their transferable skills cursory consideration. Even if they award themselves credit for functional skills, they often assume their accomplishments are so unrelated that they can't be transferred into viable selling points.

Career changers often brood about forsaking their expertise. They contemplate their years of education and experience and feel guilty about wasting the valuable knowledge they have accrued. They worry about their income plunging—never to regain its previous level. They fret about their identities. And even though they desperately want to, they have difficulty believing family and friends, who say the power, prestige and compensation they derived from their former positions aren't important.

If you're having these feelings, it may comfort you to know that other career changers are experiencing them, too. Unfortunately, knowing that you aren't alone doesn't help you to write a resume.

Points to Ponder

To start a new career, you must decide that tomorrow holds the promise of a fresh and exciting future. You'll need to put aside your former career's persona and concentrate on the skills and achievements from your paid and unpaid experience that relate to your new occupation.

A few years ago, Darryl Canterberry, a professor of anthropology, decided to move from academia to "the real world." To make the transition, he sought help from a career planner, who guided him through a series of exercises to identify his ideal career. After talking to a number of people and conducting library research, Darryl decided he would make an excellent sales or customer service representative for a company expanding into Latin America. He was confident about his decision because he spoke both Spanish and Portuguese, had many contacts in Central and South America, and possessed excellent interpersonal and research skills.

To prepare himself for job interviews, Darryl worked with the career planner to construct a resume that highlighted his salient experiences in international business, banking, and relief efforts and his uncommon understanding of cultural and business mores in Latin America. After much effort, he finally finished the resume.

But when Darryl reviewed it, he felt panicky. The person the resume described was a stranger! When his counselor saw the expression on his face, she asked what was wrong. He told her he couldn't use the resume because it described someone else. The counselor smiled and systematically pointed to each achievement saying, "Did you do this? And this? And this? And this?" Sure enough, Darryl answered yes to every one of them.

A few minutes later, he had a revelation. He realized that instead of being an academic, he was now an international business executive. All his volunteer and paid experience working with the World Bank, arranging for archaeological expeditions with Latin American officials and helping governments to coordinate resources for hurricane and earthquake relief efforts gave him a tremendous edge that few other people in his city possessed for doing business south of the border.

Armed with the conviction that he had something substantive to offer, Darryl concentrated his job-search efforts on companies selling heavy equipment products and services internationally. After a few months, he landed a customer service position at Jet Fleet, a firm that leases and maintains corporate jets. During his first year there, he doubled its service contracts.

Before Darryl could discuss his value to potential employers, he had to convince himself he was marketable. If you are grappling with this issue, use the transferable skills inventory from Chapter 2 (just like he did) to summarize the activities and functional skills that are most adaptable to your new career.

While our business culture places a priority on specialties, functional skills are actually more salable because they are useful in a variety of contexts. High-level positions demand more transferable skills than entry-level ones: The farther you progress in an organization, the more of a generalist you must become. When IBM's Board of Directors chose its new CEO, they selected an executive from an entirely different industry. They were more interested in his ability to "reengineer" a company than in his knowledge of computers.

If you investigate the requirements of any position, then match them with related activities from your skills summary, you will have a better-than-average chance of eliciting an interview. Since so few people take the time to tailor their experience to their job objective, your resume will stand out from the others. And even if your background isn't as relevant as the competition's, customizing your resume will make you seem more qualified, especially if other applicants mail generic resumes.

Employers want colleagues who can solve problems or bring new options to the table. If you have discovered an organization's most pressing opportunity or problem and have ideas about how to resolve it, a hiring manager should be eager to discuss how your skills and experience can benefit his company. If you do a credible job of addressing a manager's needs on paper, he'll give you the chance to discuss the details in person.

As a career changer, you must be careful to choose a resume format that showcases your experience effectively. A chronological format can do more harm than good because it focuses on experiences you want to minimize. If you spent the bulk of your career in banking, and want to switch to nonprofit management, listing your experience by job title will only accentuate your banking background. On the other hand, if you categorize your background by function, you can reduce the emphasis on your old career and direct readers' attention to what you can do for them. If you decide on this approach, a hybrid or functional format will probably serve you better than a chronological one.

Although a functional format works well for career changers, play devil's advocate and consider the potential benefits of using a chronological approach. Suppose you have spent several years supervising the continuing education department of your local community college, but you would like to be a training and development manager for a corporation. While most professionals would call this a career change, the two positions have some strong parallels. Because your old and new job responsibilities are similar, a chronological format may be to your advantage because a human resources recruiter is more comfortable with it and:

☆ Your current position obviously gave you significant experience in managing an educational function for adults.

☆ Many corporations use college or university continuing education courses for their employees.

☆ A recruiter will know that you're familiar with assessing training needs, developing programs to fit specifications, convincing students to take courses and evaluating and revamping curriculum as needed.

☆ A potential employer knows your management position requires you to generate annual budgets, hire and supervise staff, interact with other department managers about common issues and advocate strategies with high-level managers.

If you state how your achievements in your current position might be beneficial in your new job, a potential employer should get the point.

As in any resume, your education section should relate your academic credentials to your job objective. If your major isn't compatible, delete it, stating only your degree level and institution. If you want to switch from accounting to a more people-oriented profession, use "BSBA, University of California at Berkeley" rather than "BSBA, Accounting, University of California at Berkeley."

It's also wise to discard specialized continuing education courses that are pertinent only to your former career or company. But include training in generic skills, such as WordPerfect or Lotus, that are always in demand.

Also omit irrelevant professional organizations. If you're a teacher who plans to change careers, leave out your membership in the National Education Association because very few businesspeople belong to it. On the other hand, if you are a state or national officer of the NEA and widely known as an advocate for collaborative programs between education and the private sector, be sure to mention it.

Example Resumes

Sue Carpenter

Sue Carpenter is a world traveler with a successful track record in both profit and nonprofit organizations. Having recently spent several lucrative but unhappy years in financial services, she decided to return to the public sector. In her networking to identify potential career opportunities, she found two that particularly interested her: account executive with the business and professional institute of the local community college district, and branch director for the YWCA. She has written two completely different resumes for these openings, one hybrid and the other chronological. Why do you think she did this?

Sue decided to use a chronological resume for this position for three reasons:

☆ Her last job was a marketing rep for a service provider, so it has many similarities to her new objective.

☆ Because she'll be selling to business professionals, she wants to emphasize her recent experience in that role.

☆ All of her other positions were with educational institutions. The one in Yokohama had cache. Her instructor role with another community college district indicates her familiarity with that environment, and her Aquathenics experience combines both sales and management.

Chronological Resume

SUE E. CARPENTER
702 Sabrina
Lakewood, MA 02332
(617) 419-7818

OBJECTIVE   Account Executive with the Business and Professional Institute of the Monmouth County Community College District.

EMPLOYMENT

Marketing Representative (1993–present)
Baldwin Financial Group
Boston, MA

— Sold insurance, mutual funds, and real estate limited partnerships to businesses and individuals.
— Developed a marketing plan to reach desirable prospects.
— Cold called 40 prospects a day either by phone or in the field.
— Completed a 5-week training program in sales techniques.

Pension/Profit Sharing Specialist (1988–1993)
RepublicBank, Dallas
Dallas, Texas

— Provided support to one Trust Officer. As a team we were responsible for 150 accounts totaling $164 million in assets.
— Evaluated investment needs of clients and implemented investment options.
— Directed assets to proper accounts through wire transfers, direct trade confirmation or written instruction to the Accounting Department.
— Supervised an average of three allocations per week.
— Calculated 25 termination benefits per week.
— Responded to 30–40 telephone contacts per day.

Athletic Director, Physical Education and Home Economics Instructor (1983–1988)
Yokohama International School
Yokohama, Japan

— Developed and implemented curriculum in two subjects for 300 students grades 1–12.
— Evaluated student performance; lectured to groups; advised individuals; fostered a stimulating learning environment; developed rapport and trust with students.
— Coordinated athletic activities; mediated between headmaster and coaches; prepared budget.

SUE E. CARPENTER — 2

Instructor of Consumer Education (1982–1983)
Rancho Santiago Community College District
Santa Ana, California

— Directed and taught consumer education programs to low-income adults.
— Developed curriculum that was adaptable to a diverse audience using visual communications to illustrate principles.

Marketing Director, Assistant to Founder, and Instructor (1977–1982)
Aquathenics
Long Beach, California

— Sold water exercise programs to 12 municipal recreation departments in Southern California.
— Hired and trained 10 instructors.
— Maintained financial records.
— Marketed program extensively throughout California establishing new classes, recruiting instructors, evaluating existing classes.

EDUCATION

1993	Completion of NASD exams, Series 63 and 22
1989	Certificate of Employee Benefits Specialist (CEBS) courses: Pension Plans and Asset Management
1982	MA Home Economics with Family Finance emphasis California State University, Long Beach
1980	BS Recreation Administration California State University, Hayward
1982–88	Extensive travel in Far East, Australia, Nepal, and Europe

ACTIVITIES

Member, Downtowners Toastmasters, Dallas
Member, International Folkdance Coop
Member Downtown YMCA Squash League
Avid Sailor and retired marathoner

REFERENCES

Available on request

Every one of her former jobs reinforces why Sue would make a good account executive for a community college.

This resume is a hybrid format because:

☆ Sue's two most recent jobs had little to do with managing a YWCA. Using a chronological style would have buried her most relevant experiences on the second page of her resume.

☆ By listing her achievements by function, Sue emphasizes the specialized knowledge from her profit, nonprofit and volunteer experience, which mirror the responsibilities of a YWCA branch manager. These include everything from water sports to crisis counseling, folk singing, home economics, public speaking and cultural diversity.

☆ Sue has a good deal of management experience from her various careers. Under decision making skills, she mentions her background in supervising staff, marketing programs, budgeting and administering funds, raising money, designing facilities, and evaluating and recommending options. Combining all skills into a concise format would have been much more difficult using a chronological model.

Hybrid Resume

SUE E. CARPENTER
702 Sabrina
Lakewood, MA 02332
617-419-7818

OBJECTIVE   A director's position with the YMCA using my decision making, communication and people skills.

EXPERIENCE

Decision-Making Skills

— Coordinated 12 athletic programs involving 300 participants at the interschool, intramural and extracurricular levels.
— Marketed a water exercise package to 10 municipal recreation departments, YMCAs, and private clubs throughout California. The package provided a water exercise program, instructor, publicity assistance and all administrative and financial bookkeeping.
— Administrated 150 retirement plans totaling $164 million as a team with one Trust Officer.
— Evaluated financial investment needs of clients and implemented investment options.
— Designed and supervised construction of a home economics classroom.
— Prepared budget for physical education department.
— Raised $3,500 for gymnasium project by running a full marathon and collecting on pledges.

Communication Skills

— Developed curriculum adaptable to a diverse audience using visual communications to illustrate principles.
— Planned two workshops for employee benefits staff.
— Conducted evaluation workshop for public speaking club members.
— Hired and trained 10 water exercise instructors.
— Mediated between headmaster and coaches.
— Coached three intermural sports during the school year.
— Sold insurance and mutual funds to businesses and individuals by cold calling 40 prospects a day by phone or in the field.
— Competed in four regional speech contests.
— Performed in a folk-singing group.

People Skills
— Taught consumer education to Spanish-speaking adults, adapting course content to suit particular needs.
— Taught water exercise in classes of 12–30 adults.
— Counseled individuals in a family financial crisis clinic who felt they were on the verge of bankruptcy.
— Fostered a stimulating learning environment.
— Developed rapport and trust with students.
— Taught two diverse subjects to 300 international students grades 1–12.
— Volunteered in free health clinic assessing patient need and assisting medical staff.

EMPLOYMENT CHRONOLOGY

1993-present	Marketing Representative Baldwin Financial Group, Boston, MS.
1988–93	Pension/Profit Sharing Specialist RepublicBank, Dallas, Texas
1983–88	Athletic Director, Physical Education & Home Economics Instructor Yokohama International School, Yokohama, Japan
1982–83	Instructor of Consumer Education Rancho Santiago Community College District, Santa Ana, California
1977–82	Area Director, Instructor Aquathenics, Long Beach, California

EDUCATION

1982	MA Home Economics with Family Finance emphasis California State University, Long Beach
1980	BS Recreation Administration California State University, Hayward
1982–88	Extensive travel in Far East, Australia, Nepal, and Europe

ACTIVITIES

Member, Downtowners Toastmasters, Dallas
Member, International Folkdance Coop
Member, Downtown YMCA
Member, American Society for Training and Development
Avid sailor and retired marathoner

Military Resumes

Professionals leaving the military represent a large group of careers changers who have a host of marketable skills and relatively little information about how to promote themselves to civilian employers. On pages 224–226 are two resumes written by former officers who are pursuing very different careers. One is interested in administrative management; the other wants a position in high-tech sales or marketing support. Both have chosen a functional approach to highlight their achievements and de-emphasize their military backgrounds. However, they've listed courses obviously provided by the armed forces which relate to their new careers.

Military Resume

Davis Fisher
27 Coral Cove
New Haven, CT 06515
203-461-1718

OBJECTIVE

Administration management position.

BACKGROUND

Twenty-two years of problem solving, decision making, upward movement and increasing responsibility. Extensive hands-on experience administering, planning and managing operations in the following functional areas: facilities management, purchasing, personnel/staff development, financial management, management information, program management, logistics, maintenance, transportation and telecommunications.

PROFESSIONAL EXPERIENCE

Facilities Management
— Planned, coordinated with principals and successfully completed a physical relocation of 75 people and equipment resulting in minimal disruption to service and measurable improvements to work flow.
— Managed eight-person staff responsible for administrative support services and helped facilitate rapid expansion; growing the organization from 250 to 800 people with no increase in staff and 95% customer satisfaction.
— Orchestrated consolidation of supplies and equipment in storage resulting in a 19% reduction in space requirement and $63,000 cost savings, in the first year.
— Directed a project to identify, prepare, occupy and close out administrative offices, living and dining facilities for 200 people; completing the project on time and 10% under budget.

Purchasing
— Identified requirements for supplies and equipment, sources of supply/vendors, and negotiated to select responsive/responsible bidder resulting in materials available on time at the best cost.
— Developed procedures to expedite acquisition of low dollar supplies and equipment resulting in a material receipt time reduction from five days to one.
— Implemented just-in-time motor vehicle repair parts same day purchase procedures, resulting in vehicle down time reduction from three days to one.

Personnel and Staff Development
— Assessed work load, identified critical skills, recruited, and hired qualified candidates.
— Managed organizational realignment and 100% turnover in key management positions resulting in virtually no disruption in timeliness or quality of service to customers.
— Resolved sensitive personnel problems achieving consensus with employees, unions and management.
— Developed personnel requirements, schedules, scope, content and travel plans resulting in 99% of the inspections completed on-time, within budget and to the satisfaction of senior management.

Davis Fisher   Page 2

Management Information
— Led automation improvement initiative, saving three man years in labor and $70,000.
— Instituted cutting edge bar code inventory system technology resulting in a $100,000 cost savings, the first year.

Financial Management
— Actively managed budget development, allocation and expenditures resulting in significant cost saving.
— Prepared budgets, allocated resources, monitored execution, reallocated funds and established internal controls to comply with existing policy, guidelines and constraints.

CHRONOLOGICAL EXPERIENCE

Congressional Fellowship   1991–Present

Legislative Assistant to a U.S. Senator. Analyze data, develop sophisticated positions, summarize issues, recommend key votes, create opportunity for member to achieve goals, prepare oral/written floor/committee statements and testimony, negotiate/coordinate with colleagues/congressional committees, develop bills/amendments and resolve constituent problems.

Manager of Inspections   1987–91

Directed 30-person organization responsible for conducting complex systemic inspections of personnel, administration, budget, financial management, logistics, maintenance, transportation/travel functions for a 150,000 employee worldwide organization. Determined personnel, space, equipment and supply requirements. Developed, allocated, executed and redistributed organizational budgets.

Senior Executive for Program Management   1984–87

Developed budgets, overseeing allocation, execution and follow-up. Researched and analyzed complex programs. Determined and fulfilled management information requirements.

Director of Logistics   1982–84

Directed a diverse organization of 300 administrative, purchasing, budget, supply, maintenance, transportation and quality assurance people providing support to a community of 15,000. Determined personnel requirements, managed facilities, operated office supply facility, purchased supplies and office equipment. Developed, allocated and monitored expenditures.

EDUCATION
- Bachelor of Arts, Education, Whittier College, California, 1970
- Armed Forces Staff College
- Defense Systems Management College, Program Managers Course
- U.S. Army Logistics Executive Development Program
- Specialized training: Basic Contracting Course; Graduate Level Business Accounting

MISCELLANEOUS
- Top Secret Security Clearance
- Certified Army Acquisition Manager
- Hands-on experience with IBM PC, Apple, Macintosh, WordPerfect and Microsoft Works

Military Resume

James L. Ferris
2831 Northwest Hwy.
Washington, DC 81496
202-814-9332

Objective   A sales or marketing support position with a high-tech firm.

Personal Qualifications
- ▶ Excellent at networking and building client rapport.
- ▶ Proven record in developing and conducting training programs for sophisticated systems.
- ▶ A quick learner who particularly enjoys involvement with cutting-edge technology.
- ▶ Always looking for professional growth and new challenges.
- ▶ Enjoy domestic and international travel.

Experience Highlights
- ▶ In the past year, have introduced a new product with a start-up company, a T-shirt that changes color with heat, to the Southwest. Currently serving approximately 40 accounts. This quarter sales revenues at $200,000.
- ▶ Responsible for technical support and repair to in-flight radars and computer systems on board a U.S. Navy P-3 Orion Radar aircraft.
- ▶ Provided technical support and assisted in developing a new product for Microspec, a Texas-based software firm.
- ▶ Developed a more effective system for tracking, monitoring and destroying classified naval materials.
- ▶ Taught courses in scuba diving at San Jose State University, Moffet Field Navy Base and other locations for more than 200 students.
- ▶ Spearheaded a turnaround of the struggling scuba program at Moffet Field Navy Base resulting in a 70% increase in attendance.
  - ▶ Negotiated with the Navy to cosponsor the classes.
  - ▶ Encouraged local media to promote the program.
  - ▶ Developed an advertising strategy to reach all base personnel.

Education
- ▶ Interdisciplinary studies degree in business and law. GPA:3.1.
- ▶ Navy Avionics A1, electricity and electronics schools, 1986.
- ▶ Vector marketing: sales training course, June 1989.
- ▶ Leadership and computer language courses through the Navy and University of Texas at Dallas.

Personal Data/Interests
- ▶ Honorably discharged from U.S. Navy, member inactive Navy Reserves.
- ▶ Clearance secret.
- ▶ Enjoy physical fitness, golf, scuba diving/instructing.

12

Resumes for Seasoned Professionals

Points to Ponder

If you ask a veteran careerist how his job search is going, quite often he'll say, "People keep telling me I'm overqualified. But what they really mean is I'm too old." If you ask him what types of jobs he's pursuing, he's likely to mention positions that are obviously beneath his expertise.

In effect, he's propelling himself into a nasty downward spiral of rejection and despair because he's afraid to go after hard-to-find, higher-level positions that he's better suited for. If this negative spiral continues for several months or longer, he may wonder if he's capable of performing even rudimentary jobs, let alone the ones appropriate to his level. Unless he raises his sights and develops a good support system, he's likely to succumb to the "Black Hole Syndrome," a serious psychological condition that sucks energy and hope from its job-seeker victims.

If it's just as hard to find a good job as a bad one, why not apply only for positions that will take advantage of your expertise and allow you to grow? Employers expect to see gray hair and a few wrinkles on candidates for highly responsible positions. In fact, in consulting situations, the distinguished look may be a definite plus.

Of course, there'll always be companies that offer "low-ball" salaries, recruit young turks and work their employees like dogs, but you wouldn't want to work for them anyway. And some firms discriminate against older workers to avoid paying higher benefit costs. As a general rule, organizations want to hire people who will be productive. For every manager who thinks young people work harder, you'll find another who maintains that wisdom is more valuable than a strong back. Your mission is to find the ones in the second category.

Resume research can help you do this. Investigating a company by talking to current employees and reading its annual report and trade journals will reveal important clues about its culture. For instance, if executive officers pictured in the annual report look like a fraternity composite, you can probably assume the corporation doesn't hire many recruits over age 35. But if the firm is expanding, it's likely to need an infusion of seasoned experts who can hit the ground running. If it's moving into territories where current managers have little experience, chances are it needs to hire some pros to guide the new venture.

At this juncture of your life, you may decide to do some consulting to earn income while you look for a full-time position. This option will remove you from the pool of older workers and put you into the ranks of the ageless self-employed. There's practically no age discrimination for consultants. Your biggest problem will be competing for assignments against more seasoned advisors. Suddenly you'll be the new kid on the block. Ironic, isn't it?

You might also want to start a company that accommodates a more flexible work week. Perhaps you'll select a business in an entirely different field from your former career, or investigate franchising. In either case, your age isn't critical to your success.

Whatever direction you choose, you'll need to prepare a resume that sells you to an employer, investor or client. If you choose the small business or consulting route, reread Chapter 8, which includes resumes for people in those professions. If you decide to stay in your current field, it's likely that Chapter 5, (chronological resumes) will serve you best. But if you're seizing the opportunity to make a career change, review the advice on functional and hybrid resume formats in Chapters 6 and 7.

Seasoned professionals who are seeking salaried positions should be especially careful not to write resumes that overwhelm potential employers with their many years of experience, high compensation packages or lifetime employment with one company. While none of these background facts are intrinsically bad, they may bother recruiters sufficiently to deny you interviews. To skirt these issues, use the following techniques:

☆   Avoid any mention of salary. If an ad asks you to provide a salary history, state that you're flexible or ignore the request. The recruiter will be able to tell from your experience whether your expected compensation is in the ballpark.

☆   List no more than 20 years of experience. Positions that you held early in your career usually have little to do with the job you want now, so delete them. You aren't lying if you don't mention your entire work history. Most recruiters don't care what you did when you were 25.

☆   If you have spent a number of years at one company, attach dates to each of your job titles to show your upward progression. Some potential employers might worry that you're deadwood—someone who stayed with one organization too long because he lacked the courage or initiative to try something more challenging. If you prove you took advantage of the opportunities available in your own company, you'll easily dispel this concern.

Success Stories

Marvin B. Sutton

Marvin "Bucky" Sutton is a 52-year-old technical professional in the textile industry. After being laid off, he sent out 40 resumes, had 10 formal interviews and received five job offers. His resume on pages 232–233 is a major reason his job-search campaign was so successful:

MARVIN B. SUTTON
917 Crestlodge View
Rocky Mount, SC 29210
803-433-9991
803-736-2377

OBJECTIVE   Product/Market Development Manager

SUMMARY   My varied background includes product development, process development, market development, plant engineering and customer interface in the textiles business. I am recognized for my creativity and ability to develop products and create markets by using technical, marketing and communication skills.

EXPERIENCE   **WISCASSETT MILLS**—Major high performance yarn manufacturer for industrial and apparel applications.

Development Manager, Albemarle, NC (1991–Present)
Responsible for product and market development.

- Expanded business 25% by developing products for industrial and apparel end uses.
- Managed programs resulting in 50%–300% improvement in margins implemented into innovative niche businesses.
- Introduced two new high-performance fibers from product specifications through customer support and acceptance.

HOECHST CELANESE—$25 billion multinational manufacturer of fibers, plastics, chemicals and pharmaceuticals.

Senior Development Engineer, Charlotte, NC (1987–1991)
Responsible for new end-use product development for innovative applications of PBI fiber.

- Managed development resources for new thermally protective industrial products that doubled the number of marketed end uses.
- Introduced PBI into the industrial laminated fabric area including laminated PTFE, aluminized and neoprene coated fabrics.
- Engineered test equipment evaluating end-use product performance thereby strengthening the company's competitive advantage.
- Used communication skills as technical spokesman at seminars, authored technical papers and marketing bulletins, and earned a solid reputation of technical competence and integrity for the company.

MARVIN B. SUTTON   **Page 2**

Senior Plant Engineer, Rock Hill, SC (1981–1987)

- Managed plant engineering services for a $32 million new fiber plant start-up that was completed on time and within budget. Resin and fiber processes include polymerization, dope preparation, spinning and drawing.
- Supervised in-house and contractor support to implement design, fabrication, installation and commissioning of $4.5 million in equipment improvements.
- Engineered the control strategy, software development, installation and commissioning of a plantwide computer system that manages all major process functions.

Project Engineer, Greenville, SC (1976–1981)

- Pioneered a sitewide quality control computer system that accelerated the quality control decision-making process by automating data collection.
- Innovated microprocessor based textured yarn monitor equipment resulting in fewer customer complaints.

Project/Quality Control Engineer, Shelby, NC (1969–1976)

- Patented process for colored polyester and high-tech polyester finishes.
- Responsible for engineering and development aspects of nylon and polyester spinning and drawing processes.

EDUCATION   BS, Chemical Engineering, North Carolina State University, Raleigh, NC.

PROFESSIONAL   National Fire Protection Association (NFPA)
American Institute of Chemical Engineers
ASTM
S.A.F.E.R. & F.I.E.R.O. (fire service organizations)

INTERESTS   Golf, competitive speaking, director of NAIC, Toastmasters International.

Bucky offers some tips for other seasoned job hunters. While they represent a simple, commonsense approach to job hunting, their impact can be profound. Put this list in a convenient spot where you'll see it often.

Bucky's List

Be enthusiastic! Be honest with the employer and yourself. Know what you want. Be assertive. Maintain your sense of humor. Be dedicated to the search but be reasonable—it can't be done eight hours a day. Reward yourself when you have a successful interview.

Step 1   Network, network, network.

Step 2   Seek professional help.

Step 3   Get leads from networking, help-wanted ads and headhunters.

Step 4   Know the company before contacting it.

Step 5   Find out what the employer wants.

Step 6   Write a resume that fits the employer's needs.

Step 7   Send out resumes and follow up.

Step 8   Follow up with headhunters.

Step 9   Practice the interview.

Step 10   Control the interview.

Step 11   Perform a self-evaluation.

Step 12   Reward yourself for a successful interview.

Peter A. Wilde

Peter Wilde became unemployed after his company of 18 years ceased operations. The following resume helped him land an interview for an opening at KAR Products, a full-service distributor of maintenance and repair products for industrial, fleet and automotive markets. He beat out several hundred other candidates for the position as manager of special products.

In Peter's case, the keys to writing a successful resume include:

☆ Not dating himself by limiting his background to 15 years of experience.

☆ Providing the results of each of his accomplishments.

☆ Making his resume readable and having it printed on fine bond paper.

☆ Asking knowledgeable friends to critique the resume's content and layout.

PETER A. WILDE
27 N. Mockingbird Lane
Liberty, Illinois 62702
309-763-8864

OBJECTIVE
Seeking Marketing position using my knowledge, experience and skills in marketing and sales publications to support field sales force and distribution network.

PROFESSIONAL BACKGROUND
Fiatallis North America, Inc.   Carol Stream, Illinois
Fiatallis is a worldwide manufacturer and distributor of off-highway construction equipment with 1990 global sales over $850 million.

SUPERVISOR, MACHINERY PRICING   1986–1991
Accomplishments

Coordinated and provided quotations on requests for special, nonpublished equipment with Engineering, Purchasing, Marketing and Sales Departments and third-party suppliers.

- Generated additional $2.3 million in net revenue providing Fiatallis with $765,000 in profit during 1989 and 1990.

Created and produced two of the company's key sales tools:

- Machinery Price Manual consisting of over 40 prime products and 1,200 related options.
- Competitive Price Comparison relating Fiatallis products to over 270 competitive products by specification and price.

Developed methods and formats to determine feasibility and profitability of launching new products by incorporating specification, feature, standard cost and sale price comparisons.

- Helped to introduce 26 new models and/or series.
- Successfully developed product price strategies.

Executed special projects for management.

- Established complete price and discount structure plus price page format for direct marketing and distribution of Brazilian-built products into North America.
- Helped to assimilate complimentary product lines into the marketing mix by creating detailed price pages and aggressive price and discount structures.

Key Responsibilities

- Develop product pricing, intercompany transfer pricing and standard costs.
- Supervise staff of two and oversee maintenance of price and cost systems.
- Assist in business planning and assessment of margin effects of price and discount modifications.
- Assist in domestic, governmental and international bids.
- Administer price adjustments and discount schedules.
- Generate product and accessory margin analyses.
- Actively participate in Product Launch Committee.

SENIOR PRICING ANALYST

Prepared international market and pricing studies, special product studies and quotations; developed business plans and assisted in designing and publishing price manuals and price comparisons.

- Developed procedure for establishing costs for imported products, improving accuracy in business plans and margin analyses.
- Supported the introduction of 33 new models and/or series, providing timely product information to aid dealer network and field sales force.

EARLIER EXPERIENCE

Held positions in Order Administration including Contract Analyst and Supervisor, International Order Entry. Processed orders with domestic manufacturing facilities from offshore distributors and dealt with import licenses and letters of credit.

- Created international order processing procedures.
- Managed multimillion-dollar contracts with Russia and the Middle East.

EDUCATION

Bachelor of Science, History, Carroll College, Waukesha, Wisconsin.
American Management Association courses in management and pricing.
Fiatallis-sponsored Advanced Sales Seminars.
Working familiarity with Microsoft Excel 3.0.

Lawrence George

Larry's case is similar to those of thousands of highly productive professionals who assume they have implicit contracts with their organizations until retirement, then are suddenly terminated due to a corporate downsizing, merger or hostile takeover. Fortunately, since so many "Larrys" are looking for jobs, it's no longer a stigma to be unemployed.

This former CFO is taking a two-pronged approach to his job search. He's investigating the viability of starting his own consulting business and interviewing for CFO positions at medium-size firms that have good growth potential and may go public in the near future. He works on his search at an outplacement facility four days a week and considers his job search his job. But, like the Larry mentioned in Chapter 1, he is spending more time with his family, playing golf often and completing special projects he put off for years.

Larry has prepared an excellent resume, starting with a clear objective. He has quantified and emphasized his accomplishments, used action verbs, and minimized his "one company" career. However, his resume doesn't follow all the usual guidelines. He has listed his education before his experience and shown all the jobs he's held in his career. Even though he knows the rules, he has consciously chosen not to follow some of them because he thinks the combination of his business and high-tech degrees is important enough to warrant prime space and because he doesn't trust people who delete portions of their backgrounds. He is exercising his prerogative to break rules that disagree with his personal philosophy. If mentioning more than 20 years of experience disqualifies him for consideration, that's OK with him because he values his integrity.

If you find yourself chafing against some of the guidelines in the book, trust your instincts. Resume writing is part art and part science. You're entitled to bend or break any of the rules if you have good reason.

LAWRENCE GEORGE
2392 Northwood Lane
Boise, Idaho 83703
Off: 208-881-1301
Res: 208-142-7964

OBJECTIVE   **CHIEF FINANCIAL and ADMINISTRATIVE OFFICER** where my strengths in administration, analysis and presentation will improve staff efficiency and management effectiveness.

QUALIFIED BY   Over 20 years of broad-ranging experience, including two periods of rapid growth and numerous acquisitions. Particularly adept at straightforward communication, capturing the essence of complex subjects and getting the job done right the first time. Skilled in financial analysis, administration, investor relations and human resources in addition to traditional CFO responsibilities.

EDUCATION   MBA, Management, Pennsylvania State University
BS, Aerospace Engineering, Pennsylvania State University

Professional Accomplishments at Grace Energy

Grace Energy is a diversified energy company with $500 million in sales operating through six autonomous divisions. It went public in 1989 with 17% of its stock in a $90 million offering led by Merrill Lynch and Salomon Bros.

- Directed the efforts of Grace staff and coordinated the activities of investment bankers and operating divisions in the "due diligence." Prepared the prospectus and the road show presentation and was one of the four road show participants in 14 cities in the United States and Europe.
- Built a quality investor relations program from scratch and later hired a top-notch investor relations VP recruited from a giant competitor. Designed charts and gave presentations to groups of analysts and one-on-one to key investors around the country. Increased coverage from 2 analysts to 10 and "retail" ownership from 5% to 25%.
- Designed management information and public reporting systems including detailed monthly spreadsheets and variance explanations, annual budget/forecast spreadsheets and presentation charts, quarterly reports and the annual report to stockholders.
- Prepared extensive board requests for over 100 acquisitions and asset purchases ranging in size from $1 million to $100 million during 1975–1981 and 1986–1989.
- Designed annual and long-term incentive programs, linking awards to specific financial objectives unique to each operating division.
- Presided over the closing of our 60-person Boise corporate office. Designed the severance policy, hired an outplacement firm and set up program to explain termination schedule and benefit plan options to employees.

LAWRENCE GEORGE
Page Two

Professional
Experience

Grace Energy Corporation, Boise, Idaho
Senior Vice President and Chief Financial and Administrative Officer.
Responsible for Investor Relations, Human Resources, Economics and Legal
functions in addition to Accounting, Tax, Treasury and Financial Planning.
Directly managed staff of 60 people with annual overhead budget of $10
million. Set policy and example for several hundred financial employees in six
divisions. Served as Chief of Staff to Grace Energy President (and effective
CEO) in all aspects of strategic planning and operations. (1986–present)

Vice President Financial Planning. Managed annual and long-range
planning, prepared all capital expenditure requests, acquisition analyses,
competitor studies, management reporting and analysis. Managed 6–10 MBA
financial analysts in addition to MIS, Word Processing and Reproduction
departments. (1978–1985)

Manager Financial Planning. Supervised financial analysts and assisted in
managing MIS, Word Processing and Reproduction departments. Designed
100+ column spreadsheets for each of 10 divisions for monthly reporting of
key industry data and Grace Energy financial results. (1975–1977)

Recreational Vehicles Division, W.R. Grace & Co., Los Angeles, California
Manager Financial Planning and Analysis. Prepared budgets, capital
expenditure requests, operating variance analyses, competitor studies and cash
flow projections. Two companies, Shasta and Fan Coach, produced travel
trailers and motor homes in 10 U.S. plants. (1974)

Footwear Group, W.R. Grace & Co., New York, New York
Controller. Reviewed budgets and capital requests. Performed consolidations,
summaries and divestment analyses, and prepared board charts. Performed
"what-if" calculations on an acquisition "kicker" formula. Analyzed operating
results for the group executive and participated in monthly meetings with the
chairman. Business included three shoe importers, a domestic manufacturer and
a 34-store retail shoe chain. (1972–1973)

Other Relevant Experience:

Senior Financial Analyst, Corporate Office, W.R. Grace & Co., New York,
New York (1970–1972)

Financial Analyst, Corporate Office, General Dynamics Corp., New York,
New York (1969–1970)

Budget Analyst, Fort Worth Division, General Dynamics Corp., Fort Worth,
Texas (1967–1969)

"I don't care if you *can* break into our mainframe computer . . .
we're not hiring any programming engineers right now!"

13

Electronic Resumes

No book on resume writing in the 1990s would be complete without a chapter on how to deal with the emergence of computerized applicant-tracking systems and job databases.

So far, these high-tech alternatives to the traditional "resume-in-an-envelope" approach are catching on primarily at major corporations. That's because big employers are so deluged with resumes that they need some way of reviewing them without intense human intervention. By using a computer to pick out keywords from an applicant's resume, they can find the equivalent of a needle in a haystack; for example, a geologist in northern Wisconsin with 15 years' experience earning $53,000 annually who's willing to relocate. By typing in a few keywords (geologist, Wisconsin, 15 years, $53,000, relocate) into a computer-tracking system or job bank, the company can narrow its search instantly.

Grabbing attention, however, means you have to create a resume that's designed to be scanned into a computer system. For advice on succeeding in this effort, I contacted two of the nation's experts: California career columnist Joyce Lain Kennedy and business editor Thomas J. Morrow, coauthors of the books *Electronic Job Search Revolution* (New York: John Wiley & Sons, 1994) and *Electronic Resume Revolution* (New York: John Wiley & Sons, 1994).

According to Kennedy and Morrow, computers read resumes differently than people do, and they're making it much easier for employers to comparison-shop among job seekers. If there's a hairbreadth's difference between candidates, computers can split it. They compare every measurable differential and shade of meaning in experience, skills, education, previous employers and career achievement.

In fact, computers are doing for employers what giant shopping malls have done for consumers. Instead of running all over town to one merchant here and another there, trying to remember what one is offering and the other isn't, shoppers can now move back and forth quickly among stores and their competing neighbors. The shopping mall competition has sharpened consumers' bargaining awareness and buying power.

Similarly, employers operating computers armed with the right software can compare notes on thousands of applicants in an instant. Millions of candidates today are being entered into hundreds of automated applicant-tracking systems that are similar to the theater industry's casting directories. They're being used by employers and executive search firms, and by independent resume databases operated by commercial enterprises, colleges and the federal government. The technology is rewriting the rules on how to find jobs in the 1990s.

Fourteen Power Tips

It isn't every day you write a resume specifically for a company with a computer-scanning system. But how well you do it can affect your future since so many companies now rely on these systems. In this new age of marketing yourself electronically, here are 14 power tips from Kennedy and Morrow that can make the difference between a languishing job hunt and one in which you capture a position you love:

1. Cover Letters

For all jobs, include a cover letter with your resume. Some recruiters of junior-level personnel say cover letters aren't used for anything except slipsheets to separate a stack of paper resumes before they're fed into a scanning system.

Most recruiters, however, say they want cover letters to amplify the resume and will store them electronically along with the related resumes. Always include a cover letter when aiming for a top-management job or responding to an ad.

Until you become a viable candidate for a specific position, chances are your cover letter won't be reviewed. But once you make the short list, recruiters want to retrieve every scrap of information about you.

Your cover letter should herald your most impressive and relevant qualifications. If you're responding to a help-wanted ad, be sure to echo in your cover letter as many key words from the ad as you legitimately can.

A cover letter also is a good place to tell the recruiter how you happened to send a resume. Here's what a top corporate recruiting executive, who wishes to remain anonymous, says on the topic of cover letters:

"In computer systems we considered, you can select a source for the resume. For example, it may have been generated by an employee referral, customer referral, executive referral, newspaper advertising, job fair, and so forth. It's helpful to us if we know how you found out about the opening, or who referred you. If I place a $5,000 ad in the *Los Angeles Times,* I want to know how many resumes I got for my money. With our systems, I pull monthly reports that track where resumes are coming from. When I can't determine a source, I code it as 'U.S. Mail,' which to us means unsolicited. If I was reviewing a resume that started, 'Ben Hooks of the NAACP suggested that I send you my resume,' the statement would get my attention. If I coded it as 'NAACP' and was doing special recruiting, I might search that source code first."

2. The 85 to 90 Percent Rule

At Abra Inc., a major software company in St. Petersburg, Florida, product manager Dan Harriger gives insights as to why you should stick to vanilla resumes—without lots of graphics and fancy fonts—especially when you're applying for a job many others can fill as well as you.

"The password in computerized resume processing is percentages," he explains. "As an example, an employer who receives 4,000 resumes in a four- to six-month period prior to hiring seasonal employees needs to scan only 85% to 90% of them with a good degree of accuracy. Within those boundaries, the employer will find plenty of qualified candidates."

What about the 10% to 15% of resumes that come out looking like alphabet soup after a computer scanning? "They lose. Resumes with garbled text aren't corrected by hand because they're not needed. It's a waste of time and money when plenty of qualified candidates are being found by using the 85% to 90% rule," he explains. His advice: Think in terms of no-frills resumes.

3. Looking for a Concept

Just as you color-coordinate your wardrobe, look for unifying themes for your resume. Choose a concept, then use it as a reminder to give specific examples of your skills. To illustrate, the function of marketing is a concept; trade shows, marketing research and focus groups are the examples. Human resources is at the concept level, while employee benefits, 401(k) plans and compensation analyses are at the amplification level.

Consciously focusing on a concept helps you stay on track without wasting space on nonproductive and irrelevant information.

4. Qualifying Problems

If age (too much of it) is your job problem, omit years just as you would on a paper resume. Use only your past 10 to 15 years of work history. A computer won't care, and your resume won't be electrocuted because it doesn't have this information. What happens when it reaches human eyes is another issue.

If you need to indicate that you're completing a college degree or other credential, or that you have the equivalent of the appropriate credential, don't make the mistake of putting down two dates alongside the name of an institution of higher education. To a scanning system, this is a dead giveaway that you're short of the requirements. Instead, omit a date and place an asterisk next to the school name. Be sure to place the asterisk a space away from the word, to prevent error on the optical scanner. In a footnote, write the truth: "Pursuing . . ." "Expect to complete in . . ." or "Bachelor's degree equivalent, as documented by accumulated coursework, continuing education credits and experience."

Should your problem be one of being a little shy of the requested years of experience, use only years instead of months and years. Let's say the requirement is five years' experience and you have four. You began work in December 1989, and it's now September 1994. If you show your experience as being "1989-1994," a computer will read it as five years. This treatment doesn't work when you're substantially short of the requested experience.

In case you're wondering, writing down "five years' experience equivalent" doesn't fool a computer. The systems read numbers, not words, to determine years.

5. Updating Resumes

No matter how long it takes you to find a job, keep track of the systems where your resume is lodged. Updating it every six months is recommended but, at a minimum, update your resume every year.